P

THIS IS NOT A PEACE PIPE:
TOWARDS A CRITICAL INDIGENOUS PHILOSOPHY

How can indigenous people best assert their legal and political distinctiveness? In *This Is Not a Peace Pipe*, Dale Turner explores indigenous intellectual culture in Canada and its relationship to, and within, the dominant Euro-American culture. He contends that indigenous intellectuals need to engage the legal and political discourses of the state, while respecting both indigenous philosophies and Western European intellectual traditions.

According to Turner, the intellectual conversation about the meaning of indigenous rights, sovereignty, and nationhood must begin by recognizing, first, that the discourses of the state have evolved with very little, if any, participation from indigenous peoples and, second, that there are unique ways of understanding the world embedded in indigenous communities. Furthermore, a division of intellectual labour must be invoked between indigenous philosophers who possess and practise indigenous forms of knowledge and those who have been educated in the universities and colleges of the Euro-American world. This latter group, Turner argues, must assert, protect, and defend the integrity of indigenous rights, sovereignty, and nationhood, as they are the ones able to 'speak the language' of the dominant culture while being guided by their indigenous philosophies.

This Is Not a Peace Pipe is a ground-breaking work that will encourage ongoing debate among both Aboriginal and non-Aboriginal scholars by challenging common assumptions about how best to fight for recognition of the legal and political rights of indigenous peoples.

DALE TURNER is Associate Professor of Government and Native American Studies at Dartmouth College. He is a member of the Temagami First Nation in Northern Ontario.

DALE TURNER

This Is Not a Peace Pipe

Towards a Critical
Indigenous Philosophy

UNIVERSITY OF TORONTO PRESS
Toronto Buffalo London

© University of Toronto Press Incorporated 2006
Toronto Buffalo London
Printed in Canada

ISBN-13: 978-0-8020-8016-5 (cloth)
ISBN-10: 0-8020-8016-2 (cloth)
ISBN-13: 978-0-8020-3792-3 (paper)
ISBN-10: 0-8020-3792-5 (paper)

Printed on acid-free paper

Most of chapter 3 was published as 'Liberalism's Last Stand: Aboriginal Sovereignty and Minority Rights,' in *Aboriginal Rights and Self-Government: The Canadian and Mexican Experience in North American Perspective*, ed. Curtis Cook and Jan D. Lindau (Montreal: McGill-Queen's University Press, 2000). Much of the material for chapter 4 was originally published in 'Vision: Toward an Understanding of Aboriginal Sovereignty,' in *Canadian Political Philosophy: Contemporary Reflections*, ed. Ronald Beiner and Wayne Norman (Toronto: Oxford University Press, 2000).

Library and Archives Canada Cataloguing in Publication

Turner, Dale A. (Dale Antony), 1960–
This is not a peace pipe : towards a critical indigenous philosophy / Dale Turner.

Includes bibliographical references and index.
ISBN 0-8020-8016-2 (bound)
ISBN 0-8020-3792-5 (pbk.)

1. Native peoples – Legal status, laws, etc. – Canada.   2. Native peoples – Civil rights – Canada.   3. Native philosophy – Canada.   4. Native peoples – Canada – Intellectual life.   5. Native peoples – Canada – Politics and government.   6. Native peoples – Canada – Government relations.   I. Title.

E92.T87 2006   323.1197'071   C2005-905395-X

This book has been published with the help of a grant from the Canadian Federation for the Humanities and Social Sciences, through the Aid to Scholarly Publications Programme, using funds provided by the Social Sciences and Humanities Research Council of Canada.

University of Toronto Press acknowledges the financial assistance to its publishing program of the Canada Council for the Arts and the Ontario Arts Council.

University of Toronto Press acknowledges the financial support for its publishing activities of the Government of Canada through the Book Publishing Industry Development Program (BPIDP).

Contents

Acknowledgments

I cannot possibly thank everyone who played a part in helping me create this book, but I must mention a few.

My first debt of gratitude must go to Professor James Tully. His philosophical work, wisdom, and friendship are gifts that I value greatly. The writings and lectures of Charles Taylor have been, and continue to be, important to my thinking.

Most of this book was written in the Native American Studies Program and the Government Department at Dartmouth College. I am grateful for the support of my colleagues in Native American Studies – Colin Calloway, Sergei Kan, the late Elaine Jahner, Vera Palmer, Dennis Runnels, Darren Ranco, Mishuana Goeman, Bruce Duthu, and Chris Jocks – who have critically engaged my work while enduring Anishnabi humour. Colin Calloway's work ethic is exemplary and he continues to be a role model for me. The wisdom and friendship of Vera Palmer and Dan Runnels have nurtured my intellectual and spiritual well-being, and without their support this book might not have been written.

Special thanks to my Government colleagues, both present and past, especially Lynn Mather, Lucas Swaine, Nelson Kasfir, Allan Stam, Linda Fowler, Bill Wohlforth, and Angelia Means. I'm especially thankful to Catherine Shapiro for making me feel so welcome when I first came to Dartmouth.

I would like to thank the John Sloan Dickey Center for International Understanding for their sponsorship of a manuscript review seminar that brought Melissa Williams and David Kahane to Dartmouth as external reviewers. Thanks to Walter Sinnott-Armstrong, Angie Means,

David Peritz, Lucas Swaine, and Christianne Wohlforth for their participation and thoughtful comments.

Bea Medicine, Marlene Brant Castellano, and David Hawkes have all had a strong influence on my thinking and helped get this project going.

Of course, I must mention the importance of my family to me – the Larondes, Blakes, Moores, Roys, and Pridhams. Allan and Sandra Laronde have been my best friends since childhood and I can never go too long without hearing from them. My immediate family – Terry, Ron, Ruth, and Lana – have had a positive influence on my life – who would have guessed? William made me laugh when I needed it most, and he continues to be in my thoughts.

Finally, at the very centre of my life are Stephanie, Benjamin, and Dylan. They give me strength, love, and most of all, happiness.

the passing of the pipe

passing the pipe
situated you
(little did we know
you were legislating our humanity)

smoking the pipe
unearthed ancestors
(little did you know
we never revealed our maps)

words don't hang in the air
like promises drifting
across blinding snow

our word warriors
compete in Olympian language games
wrestling in forked tongues
(with the occasional Anishnabi spoonerism)

no doubt we will still sign on dotted lines

but we now know you are
what you say
and we will
(to our dying breath)
hold you to your word.

Introduction: From Peace Pipes to Word Warriors

We are struggling with language.
We are engaged in a struggle with language.

Ludwig Wittgenstein

For better or worse, Aboriginal rights are now part of Canadian life. This has not always been the case; in fact, they have only 'existed' as constitutional rights since the repatriation of the *Canadian Constitution* in 1982. The relevant section that protects Aboriginal rights in Canada is section 35(1), which reads: 'The existing Aboriginal and treaty rights of the Aboriginal peoples of Canada are hereby recognized and affirmed.'[1] Attaching meaning and content to terms like 'existing,' 'recognized,' and 'affirmed' has been a difficult and complex road for all Canadians and especially for Aboriginal peoples in Canada. As most Canadians know, the institution that has the power to interpret the meaning of section 35(1) is the Supreme Court of Canada.[2] The Court has been attempting to add content to the meaning of section 35(1) for over twenty years, and we can now say that a 'theory' of Aboriginal rights is evolving in Canadian law.[3]

Remarkably, there are a small number of 'major' cases in Aboriginal law; however, their legal and political consequences and their effects on the quality of life in Aboriginal communities have been enormous.[4] Legal scholarship on Aboriginal rights has become a specialized field in contemporary Canadian law, and every law school in Canada now teaches at least one course on Aboriginal law. Aboriginal rights, as constitutional rights, are still developing in law; that said, one important principle is now embedded in Canadian law and politics: the meaning and content of Aboriginal rights is expressed in the legal and political discourses of the Canadian state, and therefore Aboriginal rights exist or have legitimacy only *within* the Canadian state. A slightly different way of stating this is that Aboriginal rights exist as a special class of constitutional rights that are bestowed upon Aboriginal peoples by the state and that are protected within the highest form of law in the Canadian state.

My first definitional problem among many centres on the meaning of 'the legal and political discourses of the Canadian state.' I will use this phrase to mean, broadly, the discourses of rights, sovereignty, and nationalism that are used to legitimize Canadian legal and political practices and institutions. These discourses guide the governing institutions of the state – for example, the Department of Indian Affairs and Northern Development; the Canadian legal system, including the Supreme Court of Canada; municipal, provincial, and federal political governments; the Canadian education system (from elementary schools to the professoriate); and the justice system. The content of Aboriginal rights is reasoned and articulated in a language that makes sense to those who participate in the day-to-day life of these institutions.

But many Aboriginal peoples do not understand their rights in terms that are amenable to the state's legal and political discourses. This is because many Aboriginal peoples do not perceive the political relationship as one of subservience; that is, they do not view their rights as somehow legitimated by the Canadian state. Rather, many Aboriginal peoples understand the political relationship as one of 'nation to nation.' Defending Aboriginal nationhood commits one to an 'ownership' approach to understanding Aboriginal rights. On its surface, the argument appears straightforward: Aboriginal peoples argue that they owned their lands before contact with Europeans, that they made treaties with the European newcomers to share the land, and that after contact they never gave up their claims of ownership. This view, of course, is in the minority, especially in relation to the 'within Canada' view, but it is one of the central political views defended by Aboriginal peoples. Former National Chief George Erasmus asserts that 'all across North America today First Nations share a common perception of what was then agreed: we would allow Europeans to stay among us and use a certain amount of our land, while in our own lands we would continue to exercise our own laws and maintain our own institutions and systems of government. We all believe that that vision is still very possible today, that as First Nations we should have our own governments with jurisdiction over our own lands and people.'[5]

Herein lies a fundamental disagreement between Aboriginal nationalists and Canadian sovereigntists: many Aboriginal peoples believe to this day that they own their lands, yet the Canadian state continues to assert and enforce its unilateral claims to sovereignty over Aboriginal lands. Interpretations of section 35(1) have produced a 'theory' of Aboriginal rights in Canada but have failed to reconcile these two seemingly incommensurable positions. The main reason for this failure is that the 'form' of reconciliation, if it is to occur at all, must evolve out of a very special kind of dialogue – one grounded in a renewed and more respectful legal and political relationship.

The purpose of this book is not to provide another theory or philosophical framework of Aboriginal rights. Instead, I will argue that whatever this theory looks like, if it is to be workable in Canadian society, it has to evolve out of the dialogue between Canadian *and* Aboriginal peoples. In addition, I will reflect on what it means for Aboriginal peoples to participate in this very specialized kind of dialogue and defend the following claim: *If* Aboriginal peoples want to assert that they possess different world views, and that these differences ought to matter in the political relationship between Aboriginal peoples and the Canadian state, they will have to engage the Canadian state's legal and political discourses in more effective ways. I will explore this claim in two parts.

In Part One I examine three approaches to understanding the contemporary discourse of Aboriginal rights in Canada: the 'White Paper,' 'Citizens Plus' and 'Minority Rights' approaches. Each is guided by a particular brand of liberalism that positions Aboriginal rights as part of a larger account of political justice. Besides embodying liberal forms of political thinking, these three views of Aboriginal rights purport to be accommodating Aboriginal peoples – and hence their rights – in a coherent philosophical vision of political justice. In other words, Aboriginal rights do not pose a philosophical problem for their accounts of political justice. These theories can be thought of as philosophical 'peace pipes' because they claim to respect Aboriginal peoples and their differences and to define not only the meaning and content of their rights but also their proper place in Canadian society. Part One will show that from an Aboriginal perspective, these liberal theories of Aboriginal rights are, on closer examination, not peace pipes.

Chapter 1 begins with the White Paper of 1969.[6] The recommendations it contained proposed to dissolve any form of special recognition for Aboriginal peoples. The White Paper's stripped-down view of equality would have rendered all citizens the same, with the state owing each citizen the same package of rights. The White Paper proposed to level the legal and political playing field in Canada so that Aboriginal peoples (then legally called 'Indians') could be welcomed into mainstream Canadian society. It offered the vision of a just society and the idea of eliminating the 'special' legal and political status of Indians and the state's fiduciary responsibilities to Indians. Indians reacted strongly to the White Paper and failed to capitulate to its proposals; this quickly propelled the political relationship into a new era.

In chapter 2 I examine Alan Cairns's 'citizens plus' view of Aboriginal rights.[7] Cairns claims that his approach represents a workable middle ground between the unjust assimilation policies of the White Paper and the 'unreasonable' claims of indigenous nationalists who demand political independence. He argues that his view of a shared common citizenship reconciles the unjust colonial attitudes of assimilationists with the unreasonable demands of indigenous separatists. I will argue that Cairns's approach fails for two reasons. First, it fails to provide good reasons why Aboriginal peoples should forget the past and accept this forward-looking view of citizenship; second, it fails to appreciate that defending Aboriginal nationhood does not necessarily make one a radical separatist. Cairns pushes liberalism beyond the narrow confines of White Paper liberalism, but his account of Aboriginal rights fails to accommodate Aboriginal people's understandings of their rights and nationhood.

In chapter 3, I examine liberal theorist Will Kymlicka's 'minority rights' view of Aboriginal rights.[8] While Kymlicka defends the Aboriginal right of self-government, he does so by classifying Aboriginal rights as a form of cultural rights rather than as rights that flow out of Aboriginal peoples' legitimate status as indigenous nations. Thus the rights of Aboriginal peoples, although they empower Aboriginal communities to some degree, ultimately gain their legitimacy by virtue of the unquestioned sovereignty of the Canadian state. Kymlicka's theory of minority rights is informative: while he defends the Aboriginal right of self-government – which is a major accomplishment in Canadian liberal thought – he does so only within a particular view of political sovereignty. For Aboriginal peoples, it matters *how* we justify the Aboriginal right of self-government – Aboriginal explanations need to play a more significant role in the theorizing of Aboriginal rights in Canada.

From an Aboriginal perspective, these three liberal theories are not peace pipes, for four reasons:

1. They do not adequately address the legacy of colonialism.
2. They do not respect the sui generis nature of indigenous rights as a class of political rights that flow out of indigenous nationhood and that are not bestowed by the Canadian state.
3. They do not question the legitimacy of the Canadian state's unilateral claim of sovereignty over Aboriginal lands and peoples.
4. Most importantly, they do not recognize that a meaningful theory of Aboriginal rights in Canada is impossible without Aboriginal participation.

Addressing the practical and philosophical issues raised by the first three objections will go a long way towards developing a rich account of Aboriginal rights in Canada. However, the fourth objection – relating to Aboriginal participation – must be resolved before we can fully address the first three. Thus Part Two of this book focuses on the problem and meaning of Aboriginal participation in the legal and political practices of the state. In chapter 4, I claim that a robust theory of Aboriginal rights must include Aboriginal voices; however, from an Aboriginal perspective, it matters precisely who these voices are that participate in the legal and political discourses of the state. The key problem of participation arises because most Aboriginal peoples still believe that their ways of understanding the world are, de facto, radically different from Western European ways of understanding the world. These differences raise a tension between Aboriginal ways of knowing the world and the legal and political discourses of the state.

The issue of participation generates epistemological problems of reconciling indigenous forms of knowledge with Western European philosophy. It also generates practical problems: How are indigenous voices to be accommodated in the legal and political discourses of the state? I contend that the intellectual work required to bring (or force) indigenous voices into the dominant intellectual community is the responsibility of a group of indigenous intellectuals called 'word warriors.' Word warriors reconcile the forms of knowledge rooted in indigenous communities with the legal and political discourses of the state. They do this for two reasons. First, our survival as indigenous peoples demands that in order to assert and protect the rights we believe we possess, we must engage the discourses of the state more effectively. Second, indigenous knowledge offers legitimate ways of understanding the world – ways that have never been respected within the legal and political practices of the dominant culture. To make matters worse, these ways have not played a significant role (except in the early treaties) in determining the normative language of the political relationship. Word warriors do the intellectual work of protecting indigenous ways of knowing; at the same time, they empower these understandings within the legal and political practices of the state. Word warriors listen to their 'indigenous philosophers' while engaging the intellectual and political practices of the dominant culture.[9]

One of the main obstacles faced by word warriors is that Canadian society, by and large, remains ignorant about the meaning of Aboriginal rights. The final report of the Royal Commission on Aboriginal Peoples (RCAP) demonstrated that Canadian society has a significant lack of understanding and respect for Aboriginal ways of understanding the world, which translates into a lack of understanding of Aboriginal rights in Canada. RCAP's recommendations centred on the claim that the Canadian state's political relationship with Aboriginal peoples ought to be renewed in the spirit of the early treaties (treaty federalism). It follows that Aboriginal peoples ought to be recognized as self-determining peoples, which in turn implies that they possess the right of self-government. In other words, the political relationship is a nation-to-nation relationship.

Claims that Aboriginal peoples possess the right of self-government, or some form of sovereignty or nationhood, have been met with scepticism and sometimes outright hostility in Canadian politics. This helps explain why, when the report was tabled in Parliament, it was immediately shelved by the Liberal government.[10] This does not mean that the report was wrong or misguided. What it says to Aboriginal peoples is that most Canadians do not understand how Aboriginal peoples fit into Canadian law and politics and Canadian society as a whole. Word warriors can play an effective role in explaining differences, while helping secure a more rightful place for Aboriginal peoples in Canadian society.

In chapter 4, I reflect on what it means for Aboriginal peoples to claim that they perceive the world differently. I also discuss how indigenous intellectuals can explain these differences. A number of indigenous intellectuals in Canada, notably Taiaiake Alfred and John Borrows, have gained some recognition in mainstream academia.[11] Their published work is bringing indigenous ways of understanding the legal and political relationship into the fields of law and political science. This kind of intellectual recognition is central to their role as word warriors; however, it is also important to reflect on the relationship that word warriors ought to have with their communities. Indigenous intellectuals have to think harder about the division of intellectual labour that will be required if we are ever to assert and defend our nationhood within the dominant intellectual culture.

In chapter 5, I discuss this division of intellectual labour by exploring three philosophical projects that are relevant to a vigorous indigenous intellectual culture:

1. *Understanding indigenous philosophy*. This project embraces indigenous thinking and world views. Ideally, these are articulated in indigenous languages (usually orally) by those who are recognized in their communities as keepers of these distinct ways of knowing the world. Put simply, the normative source of indigenous difference lies in indigenous philosophy.
2. *Indigenous intellectuals who are educated in Western European philosophy and who engage its ideas on its own terms*. This project helps indigenous intellectuals articulate their peoples' differences to the dominant culture (usually in the form of scholarly writing);
3. *Indigenous intellectuals who engage the Western European history of ideas as both a philosophical activity and a political activity*. By revealing Western European philosophy as a colonial activity, we can create a critical space for indigenous voices in mainstream academia. In this project, indigenous intellectuals engage the Western European philosophical discourses of rights, sovereignty, and nationalism as word warriors – that is, as intellectuals who assert and protect Aboriginal nationhood within Canadian legal and political practices.

These three projects, as a whole, will create what I call a 'critical indigenous philosophy.' The division of intellectual labour gives rise to both practical and philosophical problems. First, very few indigenous intellectuals are able – or even permitted – to undertake the first philosophical project: indigenous philosophies are highly specialized forms of knowledge, and not every indigenous intellectual has the right to know and articulate them. Second, there are few indigenous philosophers, and even fewer indigenous intellectuals, effectively engaging the Western European history of ideas. Word warriors explicitly engage the second and third projects, but ought to do so guided by their understandings of indigenous philosophy.[12] At this time in our development as an intellectual culture (as part of mainstream intellectual culture), our numbers are small – to the dominant culture almost insignificant – which means that we must make our intellectual labour count – *we need to be effective in engaging the existing legal and political discourses of the state.*

For us to make any successful inroads into mainstream intellectual culture, we will have to be very careful about how our ways of knowing the world are talked about, written about, and ultimately put to use in legal and political practices (such as Supreme Court decisions and public policies). Yet the 'our' I am referring to can be misleading. There is a great diversity of indigenous knowledge in the world, so we must consider making these intellectual inroads into the dominant culture *as a community of indigenous intellectuals.* In other words, our critical indigenous intellectual community would consist of intellectuals from many nations, all of them in dialogue with one another. Once our ways of thinking about the world are up for 'negotiation' in the legal and political discourses of states, we will be in the position of having to defend our world views *as legal and political arguments.* Sound arguments evolve from a series of propositions that can be shown to be true, and an indigenous intellectual community must construct these arguments so that they are coherent and most of all convincing.

This imperative may be unjust, but our survival as independent and self-determining nations demands that we bow to it. However, this reality check is met with an indigenous imperative: indigenous peoples are not going away, and they will always claim that they own their homelands. Let me return to my earlier claim: *If* Aboriginal peoples want to assert that they possess different world views, and that these differences ought to matter in the political relationship between Aboriginal peoples and the Canadian state, they must engage the Canadian state's legal and political discourses in more effective ways. The sources of these differences lie in indigenous philosophies. Word warriors must protect these forms of knowledge from exploitation by indigenous and non-indigenous peoples, and must do so mainly by engaging Western European intellectual culture. Yet at the same time they must retain strong connections to their communities.

If we want the indigenous intellectual community to benefit indigenous peoples, we must know what we are talking about in the political dialogue, and we must be clear about *what we are doing in the process*. There are no guarantees that what indigenous intellectuals do will ultimately bring about a higher quality of life for their communities. That said, indigenous peoples cannot allow the dominant culture to continue to dictate their legal and political realities. Greater participation in the state's legal and political practices is vital to our survival as indigenous peoples, but at this time in history it is by no means clear *how* we ought to participate.

Developing a more robust critical indigenous intellectual community is not going to be easy, and our attempts to navigate the intellectual landscapes will be met with resistance and even hostility (by both indigenous and non-indigenous peoples). We remain small in number, our relations with our communities are often difficult, and many of us are embedded in hostile educational institutions. The intellectual battlefield lies before us – we are still here, our ways of knowing the world are still here, and we can build on the work of past indigenous intellectuals. Through continued resistance to the hostility of the dominant intellectual culture, we will create new kinds of pipe carriers.

1 White Paper Liberalism and the Problem of Aboriginal Participation

The term person means an individual other than an Indian.

Indian Act 1880, section 12

We respect law that is fair and just, but we cannot be faulted for denouncing those laws that degrade our humanity and rights as distinct peoples.

Ovide Mercredi, Berens River

The Canadian federal government's now infamous White Paper of 1969 is often cited as one low point among many in the political relationship between Aboriginal peoples and the Canadian state.[1] For Prime Minister Pierre Trudeau's Liberal government of the late 1960s – and indeed, for many Canadians – it represented not only a viable solution to the century-old 'Indian problem' in Canada but also a just political vision of Canada. Its sponsors – notably the Indian affairs minister Jean Chrétien and his deputy John MacDonald – believed, and wanted Canadians to believe, that their proposals were going to make Canada a better and more just nation for all citizens.

For many Indians, though, the White Paper was yet another manifestation of European colonialism. Its proposals were a calculated attempt by the federal government to 'get out of the Indian business' and level the political landscape by unilaterally legislating Indians into extinction – and to do so as an act of justice. For Aboriginal peoples, justice for one culture can mean cultural annihilation for another.

In this chapter I examine the White Paper's philosophical framework (which I unimaginatively label 'White Paper liberalism') and situate it within the evolving Aboriginal rights discourse in Canada.[2] Ironically, the White Paper, although for Indians it was an exemplar of colonialism, launched a new phase in the political relationship between Aboriginal peoples and the Canadian state. The outraged response to the White Paper propelled Aboriginal leaders to demand greater recognition of their people's political rights; ultimately this gave rise to section 35(1) of the repatriated Constitution in 1982 and, more importantly, to a cluster of political positions opposed to White Paper liberalism.[3]

White Paper liberalism embodies a particular variety of a broader theory of liberalism, which has a long history in Western European political thought and practice. It is difficult if not impossible to find agreement on the meaning of 'liberalism,' but for our purposes I focus on three fundamental ideas that characterize most versions of it.[4] First, liberalism privileges the individual as *the* fundamental moral unit of a theory of justice; that is, individuals count most when we think about political justice. Second and third, but arising from the first, are fundamental notions about freedom and equality, with both attached to and measured between individuals. Liberals disagree over the 'proper' relationship between freedom and equality, but they all accept that any good theory of justice has to be couched in the language of individual freedom and equality. Other important ideas, such as those relating to tolerance and property rights, arise out of liberal theories of justice. I will say more about these as the need arises.

While I am on the topic of liberalism, there is another point worth mentioning. Our discussion of liberalism in general, and of White Paper liberalism in particular, will be in the context of a constitutional democracy. This is important because ever since the *Canadian Constitution* was repatriated in 1982, Aboriginal rights have been thought of as a 'special' class of constitutional rights. As difficult as it is for some people to believe, it does not follow from this that this is the *only* way to understand Aboriginal rights in Canada. I will show throughout this book that Aboriginal people's understandings of their 'rights' are in some ways constrained by the contemporary constitutional discourse on rights. We may not have to do away with the constitutional approach; however, I do see some serious difficulties, both philosophical and practical, with incorporating Aboriginal understandings into what I believe are the hostile legal and political discourses of Aboriginal rights.

White Paper liberalism and its characterizations of Aboriginal peoples are founded on this hostility. However, Aboriginal resistance to White Paper liberalism has undeniably helped redefine the political relationship between Aboriginal peoples and the Canadian state. Indigenous nationalists, Aboriginal sovereigntists, treaty federalists, and other defenders of the sui generis nature of indigenous forms of governance all contend that Canada's Aboriginal peoples ought to be accorded some form of unique political status.

This 'unique political status' arises from the 'special' relationship that Aboriginal peoples have with the Canadian state. There are two important dimensions to this form of recognition – dimensions that Aboriginal peoples argue are overlooked when the meaning and content of Aboriginal rights are being determined. The first is the historical relationship Aboriginal peoples had with the British Crown and later with the Canadian state. This form of recognition has continued to evolve in Canadian legal and political practices since 1982 and is articulated by the discourse of constitutional rights in general and by the discourse of Aboriginal rights in particular.[5]

The second dimension focuses on the claim that Aboriginal peoples possess a form of sovereignty, or nationhood; more importantly, the kind of nationhood Aboriginal peoples believe they still possess predates the formation of the Canadian state. One of the most serious legal issues in contemporary Aboriginal rights discourse is the problem of reconciling Aboriginal nationhood, as manifested in indigenous laws, with the Crown's unilateral assertions of sovereignty.[6]

The White Paper represented a milestone in the legal and political relationship because it was offered with genuine good will as a just solution to what clearly was a dismal situation in Canada.[7] Although the White Paper was eventually rescinded as official policy, White Paper liberalism continues to capture many of the attitudes Canadians have about Aboriginal peoples in Canadian society.

I will divide the following discussion into three parts. First I will offer a brief political context for Indian rights in Canada in the 1960s. We must remember that at the time there was no public language of indigenous self-determination, nor was there any Aboriginal right of self-government; yet there were nascent signs of an evolving discourse on Aboriginal rights in Canada. The 'trust' relationship between Indians and the federal government has undoubtedly been oppressive to Indians, but it has also provided a way for Indians to seek political and legal recognition of the rights they believe they possess.

The second section of this chapter focuses on the political, and especially the philosophical, framework of the White Paper. It is important to see the White Paper as a catalyst for shifting Indian politics in Canada. Also, examining the White Paper's philosophical framework reveals a lot about how Indians were – and in many ways, still are – accommodated within a liberal theory of justice. Many Indians reacted harshly to the White Paper, and I will examine one of the more famous responses. Harold Cardinal's *Unjust Society*, published shortly after the White paper was released, injected an angry indigenous voice into mainstream Canadian intellectual culture, which helped initiate a richer written discourse of Aboriginal rights in Canada.[8]

In the third part of the chapter I discuss four serious obstacles to generating a more inclusive theory of Aboriginal rights. I argue that these concerns – especially the problem of Aboriginal participation – need to be addressed in more Aboriginal–inclusive ways, because our understanding of Aboriginal rights and how they are implemented in Aboriginal societies ultimately affects how we understand justice in a constitutional democracy. I contend that White Paper liberalism fails to

1. address the legacy of colonialism;
2. consider that indigenous rights are a sui generis form of group rights and not merely a class of minority rights;
3. question the legitimacy of the initial formation of the Canadian state; and,
4. acknowledge that any workable 'theory' of Aboriginal rights in Canada must include the participation of Aboriginal peoples.

Unfortunately for Aboriginal peoples, White Paper liberalism remains embedded in Canadian legal and political practices and has powerful advocates at all levels of Canadian politics.[9] Tom Flanagan's recent book *First Nations? Second Thoughts* is the contemporary exemplar of White Paper liberalism.[10] Flanagan argues vehemently against the idea that Aboriginal peoples are entitled to any special rights or political status within the Canadian state. He fails to address the four shortcomings of White Paper liberalism. More importantly, he perpetuates not what he calls 'Aboriginal orthodoxy in Canada' but defends the status quo – what I call 'White orthodoxy in Canada.'

Indian Policy in the 1960s

When Pierre Trudeau came to power in 1968, Parliament was divided over how to deal with the skyrocketing costs of running the Department of Indian Affairs.[11] He ran on a platform of greater citizen participation in drafting public policy, and this especially applied to Indians.

Throughout the fall of 1968 and the winter and spring of 1969, he carried out a consultative process with Indians, with the goal of reviving the *Indian Act*. This raised hopes among many Indians that perhaps the Canadian government was finally going to do something about improving their deplorable standard of living. The consultations were extensive and represented a shift in the government's view of the place of Indians in Canadian society.[12] But then the federal government surprised everyone by releasing the White Paper in June 1969; and to make matters worse, this paper seemed not to incorporate any of the voices from Indian Country. The Trudeau government never explained why the paper was released with complete disregard for Indian participation – and many Indians felt they were owed an explanation.[13]

The paper was written primarily by the Indian Affairs Minister at the time, Jean Chrétien. It suggested a way to reconfigure the political relationship with Indians on what he claimed were more just foundations. In only thirteen pages, the report made several sweeping recommendations for changing Indian policy in Canada. The main idea of the paper was that the assimilation of Indians into mainstream Canadian society – by force if necessary – was the right approach to solving Canada's century-long 'Indian problem.' Indians were to be 'welcomed' into mainstream Canadian society, complete with all its opportunities and benefits of citizenship, and the federal government would facilitate (and celebrate) the necessary institutional processes to make that happen. In other words, the paper offered a practical way for the federal government to 'get out of the Indian business' – a relationship that was clearly not working for either Indians or the government.

No one was denying that something had to be done. The statistics from Indian Country in the 1960s spoke for themselves:

1. Indians are deplorably poor; on the Prairies their cash income is $350.00 a head.
2. Indians are deplorably unhealthy; their life expectancy is half the national average.
3. Indians are badly under-educated; their attainment is below the national average.
4. Indian housing is scandalously bad; present government programs will require a generation for correction.
5. While Indians are becoming relatively poorer, the federal bureaucracy and federal expenditures are expanding.

6. The percentage of Indians on relief is rising every year; in 1962 it was 32%; in 1965 it was 39%.
7. The government is allocating $16 million to Indian relief and something like $4 million to Indian economic development.[14]

It is important to understand just how frustrated the Canadian government and Indian peoples were, and how desperate. The government had an opportunity to gain the Indians' trust; instead, the White Paper politicized the relationship. The reaction from many Indian groups and leaders was swift, organized, and strongly critical and ultimately forced the government to shelve the White Paper and (for the time being, anyway) its explicit principles of forced assimilation.[15] Katherine Graham and Frances Abele, in their research on Aboriginal policy making in Canada for the Royal Commission on Aboriginal Peoples, wrote: 'The sense of betrayal felt by Indians and their protests, leading to the White Paper's abandonment, have been well documented. Within a year of the White Paper's release, reports commissioned by Indian organizations documented broken treaties and the repudiation of Aboriginal rights.'[16]

Before turning to the details of the White Paper, I will briefly examine the political context of the relationship between Indian peoples and the Canadian state in the late 1960s. In this post-section 35(1) era, it is easy to think that Aboriginal rights have always been part of the Canadian legal and political landscape. In fact, Aboriginal rights discourse as we know it has a relatively short legal and political history. The political relationship in the pre–section 35(1) era (1867–1982) had not changed much for one hundred years. The contemporary political relationship is characterized as a 'trust' or 'fiduciary' relationship, but the meaning of this relationship wasn't fully clarified until the *Guerin* decision in 1985.[17] For more than one hundred years the relationship was broadly characterized by

- the Royal Proclamation of 1763;
- section 91(24) of the British North America Act of 1867;
- the Indian Act of 1876; and
- The legal support of *St. Catherine's Milling and Lumber Company v. The Queen* (1888).[18]

The Royal Proclamation of 1763, in demarcating Indian Country, decreed that only the British Crown could purchase lands from Indians.

More importantly, purchases of Indian lands by the Crown *required* the consent of Indians.[19] This requirement was central to the Crown's political practices with Indians as well as basic to any understanding of the treaty relationship, and it continues to be enforced by the courts.

The British North America Act of 1867 was a unilateral piece of legislation on the part of the British Crown that created the Canadian state. Rotman tells us: 'Upon Confederation the special relationship between the Crown and the Native peoples in the newly created Dominion of Canada was given constitutional recognition. Under the British North America Act, 1867, absolute legislative authority over 'Indians, and Lands reserved for the Indians' was given to the Dominion of Canada by Section 91(24) of the Act.[20] Indians, and their lands, then, explicitly became the responsibility of the federal government. This established the fiduciary relationship at the time the Canadian state was formed.[21]

It cannot be overemphasized that the *Indian Act*, and its enforcer the Department of Indian Affairs, have always had a stranglehold over Indians. The *Indian Act* controls virtually every aspect of life on Indian reserves. Ironically, though, the *Indian Act*, while clearly a colonial policy, also prevents the federal government from stealing Indian lands. The fiduciary relationship has fostered governmental paternalism but it also protects (through treaties) what little political power Indians possess. Little did anyone realize at the time that this flicker of unextinguished political power would inspire section 35(1), and ultimately lead, for better or worse, to modern-day discussions of Aboriginal title and the right of Aboriginal self-government.

St. Catherine's Milling is an exemplary case of colonial law in that the Privy Council in England decided which kinds of rights Indians were to have over their territories without them even participating in that decision. The case involved a land dispute between a lumber company and the Ontario government. The province asserted that before the signing of Treaty 3 Ojibway lands were Crown lands, and that all the treaty did was extinguish any other interests the Ojibway might have had over the territory. The province argued that with Confederation, the province had gained control over the lands; therefore, any permits and revenues deriving from the licences ought to be regulated by the province.

The Supreme Court of Canada and, subsequently, the Judicial Committee of the Privy Council in England accepted this argument, ruling that 'the tenure of the Indians was a personal and usufructuary right, dependent on the good will of the Sovereign.' Essentially, 'a usufructuary right involves the right to use something owned by someone else, as long as that use does not destroy the thing or interfere with the rightful ownership. Hence St. Catherine's Milling determined that Aboriginal title was a "burden" on Crown title, that Crown title was underlying and preceded the signing of treaties, and that Aboriginal title could be granted and taken away by the Crown.'[22] The notion that Aboriginal title is a burden on the Crown still has not been fully purged from Canadian law. Not until the *Calder* decision of 1973 was it determined that Aboriginal title formally exists in law.

Cumming and Mickenberg's *Native Rights in Canada* (1972) was a revision of the first full study of Indian rights in Canada, which had been undertaken by the Indian-Eskimo Association.[23] Yet none of its chapters discussed the Aboriginal right of self-government, the downsizing of the Department of Indian Affairs to allow for greater political autonomy, or Aboriginal title as a constitutional right. Put simply, Indian rights as a distinctly recognized class of constitutional rights did not register on the Canadian legal and political landscape in the 1960s. Indian rights existed at the 'pleasure of the Crown.' The day-to-day lives of Indians were dictated by the unilaterally imposed colonial *Indian Act*, and the federal government was failing to live up to its fiduciary responsibilities as stated in the treaties. Life was hard on most Indian reserves in the 1960s, but there was a growing community of political leaders who were fed up with the existing relationship and determined to do something about it. Ironically, it was the White Paper that drove them to act.

The White Paper of 1969

The introduction to the White Paper begins as follows (emphasis added): 'To be an Indian is to be a man, with all a man's needs and abilities. To be an Indian is also to be *different*. It is to speak *different* languages, draw *different* pictures, tell *different* tales and to rely on a set of values developed in a *different* world.'[24]

So, although Indians are part of humanity, they are 'different' (a point stressed five times in the first three sentences). After emphasizing that these differences continue to cause Indians to live in squalor and misery, the last paragraph states: 'To be an Indian must be to be free – free to develop Indian cultures in an environment of legal, social, and economic equality with other Canadians.'

Once the concepts of individual freedom and equality have been introduced – and these are liberal principles of justice – it is a short philosophical leap to open a discussion of justice. That is, appeals to recognizing indigenous difference can be subsumed under a formal recognition of the normative concepts of freedom and equality. The new policy asserts: 'True equality presupposes that the Indian people have the right to full and equal participation in the cultural, social, economic and political life of Canada.'[25]

The report goes on to add that bringing Indian individuals into mainstream society requires the following:

- That the legislative and constitutional bases of discrimination be removed.
- That there be positive recognition by everyone of the unique contribution of Indian culture to Canadian life.
- That services come through the same channels and from the same government agencies for all Canadians.
- That those who are furthest behind be helped most.
- That lawful obligations be recognized.
- That control of Indian lands be transferred to the Indian people.

Furthermore, the White Paper states that the federal government would be willing to undertake the following initiatives to facilitate the transformation:

- Propose to Parliament that the *Indian Act* be repealed and take such legislative steps as may be necessary to enable Indians to control Indian lands and to acquire title to them.
- Propose to the governments of the provinces that they take over the same responsibility for Indians that they have for other citizens in their provinces.
- Make substantial funds available for Indian economic development as an interim measure.
- Wind up that part of the Department of Indian Affairs and Northern Development which deals with Indian Affairs. The residual responsibilities of the Federal government for programs in the field of Indian Affairs would be transferred to other appropriate federal departments.[26]

This last initiative ensured that the federal government, while officially getting out of the Indian business, nonetheless would still control what goes on in Indian Country. The normative significance of Aboriginal title had not yet explicitly become part of Canadian law, which meant that the government could unilaterally allow extinguishment to guide their proposals. At the time, the *Calder* case – a land claim initiated by Frank Calder and the Nisga'a First Nation of British Columbia, decided on 31 January 1973 – was still making its way to the Supreme Court. The Nishga Indian Tribal Council (its name at the time) sought recognition in British Columbia courts that Aboriginal title over its lands had not been extinguished. Aboriginal title at this time was still considered a 'burden on the Crown,' which meant that Crown sovereignty trumped Aboriginal title and precluded the signing of the treaties.[27] The Nisga'a lost their case by one vote, with the deciding judge basing his ruling on a technical point rather than on the merits of the case. Despite this loss, *Calder* was a milestone in federal Indian law because it embedded in law the idea that Aboriginal title exists in Canadian law and that it cannot be extinguished without 'clear and plain intent.'

Justice Judson stated in his now famous opinion: 'Although I think that it is plain and clear that Indian title in British Columbia cannot owe its origin to the Proclamation of 1763, the fact is that when the settlers came, the Indians were there, organized in societies and occupying that land as their forefathers had done for centuries. This is what Indian Title means and it does not help one in the solution of this problem to call it a "personal or usufructuary right."[28]

Three justices argued that Aboriginal title existed at one time but that it had been legitimately extinguished. Justice Hall, in his opinion, concluded that 'it would, accordingly, appear to be beyond question that the onus of proving that the sovereign intended to extinguish the Indian title lies on the respondent and that intention must be "clear and plain." There is no such proof in the case at bar; no legislation to that effect.'[29] He further argued that Aboriginal title existed in Canadian law and that in the case of the Nisga'a, it had not been extinguished. Extinguishment – or the 'Doctrine of Extinguishment,' as it is known in international law – underpins the White Paper's assumption that the sovereignty of the Canadian state is absolute.

The fiduciary responsibilities of the federal government were beginning to cost the government far too much, and senior ministers were pressuring Trudeau to make some fundamental changes in the relationship between the Canadian state and Aboriginal peoples. The White Paper was proposing a basic shift not only in the way Indian policy was

administered and financed but also in the way the political relationship
was understood within the larger Canadian state.

But what did the White Paper *say* to Indians of Canada? That is, what
was it about the White Paper that most Indians found, and continue to
find, so offensive? The White Paper contained four important messages
to Canadian society about how the Indian–Canadian state relationship
was to evolve.

*Existing Indian policies are discriminatory. The White Paper removes the
discriminatory nature of federal Indian policies and policy making in Canada.*
Indians, *as a matter of public policy*, were being treated differently, and for
many Canadians, this in itself was enough to demonstrate discrimination; furthermore, for White Paper liberals it was fundamentally unfair.
At the end of the background section, the paper stated: 'The policy rests
upon the fundamental right of Indian people to full and equal participation in the cultural, social, economic and political life of Canada ... To
argue against this right is to argue for discrimination, isolation and
separation.' A few pages later, the paper added: 'Separate but equal
services do not provide *truly* equal treatment.'[30] The kind of participation the government was calling for would have functioned in all-or-
nothing terms: all services would be available to everyone (citizens),
and everyone would be required to participate in them in the same way.

The federal government was categorizing Indians by their ethnicity
and not by their legitimate political status as indigenous nations. Services would no longer flow from separate agencies established to serve
particular groups, and especially not to groups identified ethnically.[31]
Ottawa was blind to the ownership approach; it simply could not
fathom that Indians could actually 'own' (i.e., rule over) their homelands. The language of Indian nationhood was not part of the Canadian
legal and political imagination in 1969. The kind of discrimination the
White Paper was focusing on, and that it wanted to rectify, was discrimination between different races. The 'difference' at stake was racial
difference, not political difference. There was no need to discuss Indian
understandings of treaty obligations, and fiduciary relationships arising from treaty relationships, because such obligations did not matter
as long as 'equality between individuals' drove basic understandings of
justice.[32] Rectifying discrimination between races involved levelling the
moral playing field between individuals, and doing so dissolved the
need to address controversial matters such as the meaning and content
of indigenous nationhood within a constitutional framework.

The idea of equality, especially in the framework of 'truly equal treatment,' represents a form of 'egalitarianism' that is foundational to contemporary liberal governments.[33] The government's desire to level the political playing field between individuals made sense in an era of civil rights discourse. The existing political relationship treated *individual* Indians unfairly; it followed that in freeing individual Indians, Indians as a distinct group would be freed from being a 'burden to the Crown.' The form of liberalism the White Paper embraced did not arise from a desire to accommodate differences between politically distinct peoples; rather, understandings of justice were to be grounded in the idea of equality that is embedded in the moral sanctity of the individual. Individuals, then, were to be the fundamental moral unit of justice. This is what led to the White Paper's second claim.

Indians are unequivocally citizens of the Canadian state. Since Indians are citizens, and therefore equal to all other citizens, they possess the same basic package of rights. According to the White Paper, true equality presupposed that the Indian people have the right to full and equal participation in the cultural, social, economic, and political life of Canada.[34] The idea of equal opportunity is another central idea in contemporary liberalism. In order for all citizens to be equal they must have access to the same goods, services, and institutions. Historically, Indians have not had the same opportunities as other citizens, and antidiscrimination policies have failed miserably. The state's responsibility, said the White Paper, was to remove these inequalities, and for Indians this meant eliminating the Department of Indian Affairs and Northern Development (DIAND) and all of the special programs applicable to Indians, thereby forcing them to become citizens. Forcing Indians to embrace Canadian citizenship would have two advantages for the state: first, it would eliminate discriminatory (and expensive) Indian policies, and second, Indians as Canadian citizens would be welcomed into mainstream Canadian society. Once Indians were 'welcomed' into mainstream society, they would finally leave their primitive ways behind; more importantly, they would give up their indigenous connections to their homelands. This led to the third claim.

There is no such thing as Indian nationhood. Treaty lands must ultimately be transformed into private property. With equal citizenship and opportunities comes the idea of property – another central idea in White Paper liberalism. In a constitutional democracy, citizenship implies the right to own property. Once again, the White Paper was raising the concept of 'true' equality: 'The Government recognizes that full and true equality calls for Indian control and ownership of reserve land ... Between the present system and the full holding of title in fee simple lie a number of intermediate states.'[35] No doubt, the government was fully aware that Indians were not going to relinquish the treaty relationship without resistance, so it was ready to be patient in discussing the transition from the present state of dependency to one where Indians would control their lands as private property. Regardless of how this transition occurred, the best Indians would be able to do would be to own their lands in fee simple and not in the form of Aboriginal title (never mind owning their homelands by virtue of their status as indigenous nations). This approach would unilaterally dissolve the promises in the treaties; furthermore, owning lands in fee simple would render Indians liable to municipal, provincial, and federal taxation.

Philosophical discussions about the meaning and place of property in New World politics have a long history. Since earliest contact, Indians have influenced how Europeans understand property. More importantly, Eurocentric understandings of property have sometimes been invoked unilaterally to justify the theft of Indian lands in the Americas. Only recently have indigenous scholars and intellectuals begun to unpack these understandings to show how they have been put to use to dispossess indigenous peoples.[36]

Private property is the cornerstone not only of liberal theories of justice but also of Western European economies. Even though Indians have a treaty relationship with the state, and even though the *Indian Act* still constrains life on Indian reserves, Aboriginal peoples continue to assert a unique form of ownership over their homelands. The White Paper was proposing to unilaterally extinguish the unique relationships Aboriginal peoples have with their homelands. This led to the fourth claim.

The fiduciary relationship is not forever. The federal government will make funds available to facilitate the scheduled transition from being wards of the state to full participatory citizenship. The state, by unilaterally eliminating the special status of Indians, unilaterally extinguishing the treaty relationship, and converting Indian lands to private property, would be unilaterally dissolving the fiduciary relationship. The White Paper stated: 'Those who are furthest behind [must] be helped most.' This idea of helping the 'most disadvantaged' has played an important role in contemporary political theory, especially in the liberal political thought of John Rawls.[37] The federal government could easily facilitate the transition over a finite period of time, so that at some point in the future there would no longer be a fiduciary relationship – and therefore, legally, no more Indians. The government planned to spend a lot of money in the short term in order to gradually eliminate funding for Indians entirely.[38]

It is no wonder that those Indians who believed they still owned their homelands – who still thought of themselves as indigenous nations – were so outraged at the White Paper. What started off as an almost visceral reaction to what most Aboriginal peoples deemed an unjust policy ultimately polarized Canadian politics between those who advocated some form of special recognition and those who did not. Two reactions are worth mentioning: one by a young Cree political activist whose book motivated indigenous intellectuals to become more academically active; and the other by national Indian groups who realized that they had to take political advantage of the White Paper's public failure. Below, I discuss these in turn.

Harold Cardinal's *Unjust Society*

Harold Cardinal, a young Cree political activist, wrote *Unjust Society* as an Indian response, not only to the White Paper but also to Pierre Trudeau's political vision of Canada as a 'just society.'[39] Cardinal was not so much interested in engaging in a philosophical dialogue over the meaning and tenability of liberalism as a theory of justice (although he is clear about his criticism of liberalism), as with driving home the point (again and again) that Indian voices were nowhere to be found in the government's new Indian policy initiatives. For example, he states:

> The new Indian policy promulgated by Prime Minister Pierre Elliott Trudeau's government ... is a thinly disguised programme of extermination through assimilation. For the Indian to survive, says the government in effect, he must become a good little brown white man. The Americans to the south of us used to have a saying: 'The only good Indian is a dead Indian.' The MacDonald-Chrétien doctrine would amend this but slightly to, 'The only good Indian is a non-Indian.'[40]

Cardinal further displays his anger:

> The government's proposed new Indian policy is a sick curious collage of empty clichés and distorted facts. It reflects only, but perfectly, the total lack of understanding possessed by its authors of the situation in which the Indians of Canada find themselves today. It bears more than marked

resemblance to the recent American policy of termination, which proved an utter failure.[41]

Cardinal flashes this kind of sardonic wit when he rails against the federal government's Indian policies, but the main point of his book is serious:

> The Indian must have from the federal government immediately recognition of all Indian rights for the reestablishment, review and renewal of all existing Indian treaties. The negotiations for this must be undertaken in a new and different spirit by both sides. The treaties must be maintained.[42]

It is worth making a brief digression to discuss Cardinal's point, because I believe it goes to the core of the *philosophical* differences that ground the respective political positions of Indians and Whites. The treaty position, in its various forms, takes the political stance that the treaties represent not only binding political agreements but also *sacred* agreements, and that to violate them is morally reprehensible in a political relationship between nations.[43] Most indigenous peoples have not deviated from this position. The discourses of rights, sovereignty, and nationhood are ways of 'theorizing' about what Indians are entitled to in a just political relationship. But what about explanations, or 'theories,' that flow from *indigenous philosophies*?

Herein lies a fundamental tension: the ultimate sources of Indian explanations of nationhood are found in indigenous oral traditions, yet for these explanations to be effective in Canadian law and politics they *must* be accommodated within the language of Canadian public policy. I will explore the relationship between indigenous philosophies and the discourses of the Canadian state in chapters 4 and 5; for now, I want to highlight this tension because it helps shed light on the deeply rooted anger felt by Indian leaders in the 1960s. Indians have been explaining themselves to the dominant culture since first contact, and continue to do so. Many in fact do so with an astonishing faith that the dominant culture will some day understand who we are and change the ways they 'accommodate' us within existing public policies. I believe that Aboriginal peoples must think more seriously about the constraints that are unilaterally imposed on the language we must use to articulate our legal and political goals. The fact that our ways of understanding the world are not worthy of equal participation in a dialogue over the meaning and content of *our* rights is itself a form of inequality.

Cardinal's book had a powerful impact on contemporary Aboriginal intellectuals because he raised the Indian voice against the dominant culture's stranglehold on what counted as legitimate intellectual discourse.[44] The 1960s culture of political activism allowed Cardinal to make inroads into mainstream Canadian society. The primary purpose of Cardinal's book, to me, is political; the common thread throughout his criticism is that the Canadian government has not lived up to its responsibilities and that it is about time it did so.

The problem for this generation of indigenous intellectuals is to find ways to move beyond raising angry voices and actually effect change in the dominant culture's intellectual and political culture. Writers like Harold Cardinal, George Manuel, and Wabaghesig in Canada and Vine Deloria, jr, Beatrice Medicine, and Jack Forbes in the United States all began as activists and later became intellectuals in the university environment.[45] Cardinal's book represented a watershed for Aboriginal intellectuals; their political views could now be published and read within mainstream Canadian society.

The Creation of National Indian Organizations

Another political effect of the White Paper was that it empowered four national indigenous groups in Canada: the Native Council of Canada (NCC); the National Indian Brotherhood (NIB), later to become the Assembly of First Nations (AFN); the Native Women's Association of Canada (NWAC); and the Métis National Council (MNC). For better or worse, these groups remain very much in the forefront of Aboriginal politics in Canada, and have made varying degrees of political progress with the provincial and federal governments. One problem with these groups is that they depend heavily on federal government funding. This has meant that in times of fiscal restraint, or of anti-Aboriginal sentiment in Canada (which is often), these organizations are chronically underfunded.

These groups played a consultative role in shaping the wording of what ultimately, in 1982, became the second part of the repatriated constitution. Although Indians helped shape the wording of the constitution, it is important to stress that they acted as 'consultants' and not participants in the constitutional dialogue. The first ministers (i.e., provincial premiers) sat around a table discussing the constitutional status of Indians while *our* legal, political, and philosophical experts sat behind them and listened in silence. Of course, this was the political reality that Indian leaders had to deal with at the time. For the most part, Indian leaders did the best they could. This doesn't absolve them from criticism, but it does point out that when people exist on the receiving end of a colonial relationship, there are *always* constraints on legal and political participation.

This is an important point, because it helps us appreciate – and hopefully understand better – what indigenous communities face when the dominant culture permits them to 'participate' in Western political practices. It is disheartening to see a younger generation of indigenous people criticizing their elders for signing agreements that gave up too much land or that blocked any future opportunities to assert their rights. No doubt, many decisions made then by Indian leaders are open to criticism, but when we examine more closely the conditions under which they made those decisions, it is not hard to appreciate just how difficult their position was.

The Creation of an Aboriginal Rights Discourse

The White Paper was, to most Aboriginal people, a manifestation of colonialism. However, many non-Aboriginal people believe that the liberal principles of the White Paper were fundamentally sound. The principles that guide liberalism – equality, freedom, opportunity, and especially moral individualism – have a long history in Western political thought, and the language of individual rights defines contemporary constitutional democracies. The White Paper began by focusing on the Indian as an individual: 'To be an Indian is to be a man, with all a man's needs and abilities.' The liberalism reflected in the White Paper assumed that the individual is the fundamental moral unit in developing a theory of justice and that to deviate from the sanctity of moral individualism is to lead justice off its rightful path.[46] One supposed virtue of moral individualism is that it simplifies political thinking. If every citizen of the state has the same moral worth, and if everyone must be treated equally, then opportunities to live a good life must be made available to all citizens. This brand of liberalism has been enormously influential in shaping Aboriginal public policy in Canada. What made the White Paper interesting *philosophically* is that it subsumed Aboriginal rights under its vision of a just society.

Moral individualism, though, does not simply hang in the air; it requires support or some philosophical framework to give it meaning. The fact that we live in a constitutional democracy, can own property as individuals, have opportunities to pursue a good life, and are free to choose for ourselves (within reason) what a good life is hang together with the idea of privileging the individual in a theory of justice. All of these ideas are central to a liberal theory of justice, and to understand a normative concept we must understand how it is situated within this web of beliefs. The White Paper's commitment to moral individualism was also woven into the idea that free market capitalism is the ideal economic system to frame our political understanding of justice: Indians ought to become like other citizens, which means they ought to enjoy the same rights, benefits, and economic opportunities as every other citizen in the state. As I mentioned, one recommendation of the White Paper was to disband Indian reserves and redistribute their lands (which were often treaty lands) to Indians in fee simple. In other words, Indian reserves were to be divided into individual private properties.[47] At the same time, the legal term 'Indian' would disappear (although it would be perfectly acceptable as a cultural construct), and the federal government's fiduciary responsibilities would be ended, because by then Indians would have become full-fledged citizens and taxpayers.[48]

When we incorporate the four shortcomings of the White Paper listed earlier, and weave indigenous responses into its vision of justice, we can draw four conclusions about White Paper liberalism: ⹁

- It failed to address the legacy of colonialism;
- It failed to recognize that indigenous rights are a sui generis form of group rights and not merely a class of minority rights.
- It failed to question the legitimacy of the initial formation of the Canadian state.
- It failed to appreciate that any workable understanding of Aboriginal rights in Canada must include the participation of Aboriginal peoples.

I will consider each of these points in turn.

The Legacy of Colonialism

My criticism of White Paper liberalism runs deep. One way of assessing the philosophical merit of White Paper liberalism is to situate and evaluate it within the historically defined landscape of liberal political thought and then broaden that landscape to include contemporary political thought. This is no easy task, but I believe it to be a worthwhile and necessary philosophical investigation because we have a continuing need to better understand the nature of justice, which in turn ought to have some effect on our political behaviour. But to determine the meaning of Aboriginal rights in Canadian legal and political discourses, we have to situate our investigation not only within the rich Western history of ideas but also within the context of the Canadian state's legal and political practices. The value of this kind of investigation is that it lets us explicitly address the problem of colonialism.[49]

My approach, then, is necessarily multilayered. The first inquiry engages the discourse of rights, while the second critically assesses the legal and political practices that have put the normative language of these discourses to use (especially in Aboriginal communities). I will argue that once we reconcile the normative discourses of rights, sovereignty, and nationhood with how these languages have always been used in Aboriginal policies, we will find ourselves heading towards a fair account of Aboriginal rights and a renewed and healthier political relationship.

Allow me state this in another way.

Because Aboriginal rights are a sui generis class of rights, they ought to play a sui generis role in our understandings of political justice.[50] Aboriginal rights in Canada can be understood in a number of ways; that said, there are two important dimensions to understanding them as constitutional rights. First, Aboriginal rights are part of a more general theory of rights, and their meaning is determined by engaging the discourses and practices of Canadian social and political life (law, politics, history, philosophy, and so on). The second dimension is colonialism, which is more difficult to understand and articulate, besides being even more problematic when it comes to rectifying existing policy. We cannot hope to fully understand the meaning and content of Aboriginal rights without understanding first how colonialism has been woven into the normative political language that guides contemporary Canadian legal and political practices. Colonialism has stained the legal and political relationship; its main consequence has been that Aboriginal peoples have been physically, politically, and socially relegated to the margins of Canadian society. It follows that Aboriginal voices have not participated effectively in the legal and political practices of the Canadian state. The project of unpacking and laying bare the meaning and effects of colonialism will open up the physical and intellectual space for Aboriginal voices to participate in the legal and political practices of

the state. The process of critically undermining colonialism and returning Aboriginal voices to their rightful place in the relationship between
Aboriginal peoples and the Canadian state is what I refer to as 'Aboriginal participation.'

Aboriginal participation is a precondition for generating legitimate
understandings of Aboriginal rights. Put simply, Aboriginal voices must
participate in the Canadian legal and political practices that determine
the meaning of Aboriginal rights. White Paper liberalism does not
facilitate this participation because it embraces a set of attitudes towards equality, sovereignty, and history that reinforce the view that the
recognition of Aboriginal rights is an obstacle to, not a requirement for,
a just political vision of Canada.

*Indigenous rights are a sui generis form of group rights and
not merely a class of minority rights.*

The White Paper defends a narrow understanding of equality, one
which holds that because rights adhere only to individuals, any special
form of recognition that accords rights to groups – rights that would
exist over and above what everyone else receives – must be inherently
unfair, and therefore wrong.[51] Aboriginal peoples have always asserted
that the treaty relationship situates both Aboriginal peoples and Europeans in an international type of political relationship. The disagreement between White Paper liberals and treaty federalists is not over
whether individual rights are important, or central to a theory of justice,
but rather over whether the *kind* of equality that Aboriginal peoples are
demanding (i.e., equality between legitimate political entities – nations)
can *also* play a role in our thinking about justice. The White Paper
avoids this issue by making individual citizenship the fundamental
unit of political allegiance; thus the problem of recognizing special
group rights does not arise.

The crucial question is this: Can our understanding of justice accommodate treaty federalism while preserving the normative force of moral
individualism? From defending indigenous rights as a form of group
right, it does not follow that moral individualism should be peripheral
to our understandings of political justice. As we will see in chapter 3, an
accommodation between the two forms of rights is precisely what
Kymlicka seeks. The philosophical problem is how to achieve this kind
of accommodation.

Before this accommodation can occur, White Paper liberals will have to accept that the treaty relationship embraces a richer conception of equality, and I contend that in Canadian politics, they have not yet done so. One reason why is that White Paper liberals believe strongly that the sovereignty of the nation-state is absolute and non-negotiable and that Aboriginal forms of 'sovereignty' represent a profound misuse of political sovereignty.[52] It is easy to understand why this belief is so deeply embedded among Canadians, but for many Aboriginal peoples, membership in the Canadian state is a secondary political identity.[53] The primary source of identity for many Aboriginal peoples is their community, or nation. If you ask an indigenous person in North America where they are from, most will tell you their indigenous nation first: Mohawk, Lakota Sioux, Haida, Métis, to name a few. This leads to the third problem with White Paper liberalism.

The legitimacy of the initial formation of the Canadian state is not without controversy.

The fact is, most Canadians – except perhaps for many Québécois – believe that the sovereignty of the Canadian state is a given in their lives. The idea of Canada as a country or a nation-state is so deeply embedded in Canadian society that its legitimacy is rarely questioned. It is now being questioned, but it does not follow from this questioning that the Canadian state must be dissolved. Kent McNeil, John Borrows, and other legal scholars have raised some serious legal challenges regarding the source of Aboriginal title in Canadian law, and this has legal and political consequences for Canada's unilateral assertion of sovereignty. By articulating the source of Aboriginal title, which is the right to the land itself, they are raising fundamental challenges to the legitimacy of Crown sovereignty. For example, Kent McNeil states,

> If Aboriginal title is based simply on occupation of lands by an organized society at the time the Crown asserted sovereignty, how could it be a pre-existing right? For it to exist as a legal right before the Crown acquired sovereignty, it would need to be based on some system of law, which would have to be Aboriginal, as no other law existed in North America prior to European colonization.[54]

John Borrows has recast McNeil's arguments in an indigenous context:

> A faithful application of the rule of law to the Crown's assertion of title throughout Canada would suggest that Aboriginal peoples possess the

very right claimed by the Crown. According to the Supreme Court of Canada, the rule of law consists of two inter-related legal principles: it precludes arbitrary state power and requires the maintenance of a positive legal order. Canada's assumption of underlying title and sovereignty throughout its claimed territory violates both of these fundamental principles. It is an arbitrary exercise of power aimed at dismantling Indigenous systems of law and normative order ... Canada's declaration of exclusive sovereignty over Aboriginal peoples violates the second principle of the rule of law because, in the process of this declaration, the Crown suppressed Aboriginal governance and denied these groups indispensable elements of law and order.[55]

These extracts can take us in a number of directions. The point I want to make here is that there are credible legal experts who argue that Canada's unilateral assertion of sovereignty is not without controversy and that the issues they raise are important and require addressing. Borrows's recent work has been pivotal for bringing an Aboriginal voice into Canadian legal culture. He is optimistic that indigenous legal traditions can be reconciled with a rich, empowering vision of Aboriginal rights in Canadian law. For reasons I will offer over the next few chapters, I am less optimistic. I will come back to this problem of reconciliation in chapter 5, when I examine more closely the relationship between Aboriginal ways of knowing and the legal and political discourses of the state.

Any workable 'theory' of Aboriginal rights in Canada must include the participation of Aboriginal peoples.

The White Paper does not advocate any special form of recognition for Indians, which is remarkable, considering the post-1982 constitutional recognition of Aboriginal rights. But there are contemporary defenders of White Paper liberalism. Tom Flanagan, in his recent book, *First Nations? Second Thoughts*, argues that Canada has allowed an 'Aboriginal orthodoxy' to dominate Canadian political life, an orthodoxy that RCAP's final report endorsed uncritically. Flanagan has resuscitated the White Paper and offers a series of recommendations that, taken together, would eliminate section 35(1) and force Aboriginal peoples to embrace modernity – European civilization – and assimilate into mainstream Canadian society. He claims that Indian cultures were never equal to European cultures and therefore that it is absurd for Aboriginal peoples to now believe they possess the right of self-government:

What I call the aboriginal orthodoxy is an emergent consensus on fundamental issues. It is widely shared among Aboriginal leaders, government
officials, and academic experts. It weaves together threads from historical
revisionism, critical legal studies, and the aboriginal political activism of
the last thirty years. Although its ideas are expressed in many books, it
has no Marx or Engels, that is, no canonical writers to authoritatively
define the ideology.[56]

Marx or Engels?! Beyond this astonishingly Eurocentric appeal to
Marx and Engels as 'canonical' writers, there is some irony to this
statement. Marx and Engels (especially the latter) had a more than
casual interest in the Iroquois Confederacy and appreciated the philosophical ingenuity of the Great Law of Peace as an exemplar of political
thinking.[57] Flanagan, whose book won a major academic award in
Canada, is unapologetic about his views and sincerely believes he is
right. He goes so far as to claim that his views are in the minority and
have been silenced unfairly by the majority (who constitute the Aboriginal orthodoxy).[58] Essentially, Flanagan as a White Paper liberal
wants the existing constitutional playing field to be levelled so that the
relationship can be renewed on just foundations.[59]

Yet Flanagan fails to address colonialism. It is interesting that for him,
colonialism has disappeared from the political relationship. Somewhere
between the unilateral creation of DIAND and its oppressive governing
legislation – the *Indian Act* – and the creation of Flanagan's Aboriginal
orthodoxy, Aboriginal peoples became extra-privileged citizens of the
state. From Flanagan's perspective, it is the state's responsibility to do
whatever it can to rectify any unfair distribution of rights, and such
actions make sense when it comes to Indians because of the two central
ideas of White Paper liberalism: that they are discriminated against,
and that they are citizens like everyone else. He can make these assertions about the relationship because he assumes that the individual is
the fundamental moral unit of our theories of political justice and that
these theories function within the idea that the nation-state provides the
unequivocal normative background for any discussion about justice.

These are powerful ideas in contemporary liberal discourse. Contrary to Flanagan's claim that there is an 'Aboriginal orthodoxy,' a
'white orthodoxy' in Canadian-Aboriginal rights discourse has always
existed in Canada. This white orthodoxy is characterized by the four
dimensions of White Paper liberalism: existing Indian policies are discriminatory; Indians are citizens of the state and do not possess any

special status in the political relationship; Indians do not own their lands and the treaties must be dissolved; and the fiduciary relationship must be dissolved so that Indians can be assimilated into mainstream society. For Flanagan, the Aboriginal–Canadian state relationship is not politically based; rather, the issue at hand is how 'primitive' indigenous cultures can be subsumed into the 'superior' European culture.

Flanagan invokes a clear distinction between 'primitive' and 'civilized' cultures to emphasize that European cultures are de facto superior to indigenous cultures. The 'civilization gap,' as he calls it, is more than an anthropological fact – it has political significance: 'But if one culture is simple and another complex, is not the latter also superior to the former in some sense? Increasing complexity is a hallmark of progress in scholarship and science, as well as of technical advances in engineering, commerce, and athletics. Why not in cultural generally?'[60] On page 33, he lists what he takes to be the criteria for a bona fide civilization:

- Intensive agriculture – long-term cultivation of the same ground, assisted by some combination of irrigation, fertilization, and animal husbandry
- Urbanization – permanent settlements of several thousand residents
- Division of labour among cultivators, craftsman, merchants, soldiers, rulers, and priests
- Intellectual advances such as record-keeping, writing, and astronomy. All early civilizations except the Incas developed writing, and the latter had both an astronomically based calendar and a system of record-keeping using knotted strings.
- Advanced technology. New World civilizations did not have the wheel, and their metallurgy was in the early stages, but they performed impressive feats of architecture and engineering.
- Formalized, hierarchical government – that is, a state.

Although Flanagan admits that these criteria are a matter of degree, it is not difficult to see what kind of culture he has in mind when using the term 'civilization.' This Eurocentric characterization of civil society is no accident, as it allows Flanagan to pass judgments on Aboriginal cultures, governments, and especially the Aboriginal–Canadian state relationship. For example, one proposition supporting the aboriginal orthodoxy in Canada is the claim that 'Aboriginal peoples were and are nations in both the cultural and political senses of this term. Their nationhood is concomitant with their sovereignty.' Flanagan responds

by claiming that because civil society has only one way of understanding the meaning of nationhood, 'the European concept of nation does
not properly describe aboriginal tribal community ... There can only be
one political community at the highest level – one nation – in Canada.'[61]

The idea that indigenous nations are nation 'states' represents a fundamental error in thinking about indigenous cultures, and especially
about indigenous nationhood. Flanagan's 'civilization gap' forces us to
evaluate indigenous cultures according to the standards used for mea-
suring the 'civility' of European cultures. Indigenous nationhood is a
complex concept whose meaning can only be understood by including
indigenous voices in a dialogue with the dominant culture. Flanagan
leaves no room for indigenous voices; they are not required because
from the very beginning of the political dialogue, they do not measure
up. From an indigenous perspective, what he is saying about indigenous nationhood is mistaken; furthermore, the fact that indigenous
voices are not required in order to understand the meaning of the
normative language of the political relationship means that indigenous
peoples will *never* need to participate in the relationship. This is unacceptable for indigenous peoples, and it certainly goes against the basic
principles of democracy. Contrary to what Flanagan believes, indigenous peoples make workable understandings of rights, sovereignty,
and nationhood more complex, not less.

White Paper liberalism acts as a reality check for Aboriginal peoples,
and its narrow attitudes towards Aboriginal peoples always lie close to
the surface of their relationship with the Canadian state. It often shows
its colonial face in courtrooms, in land claim negotiations, and in the
everyday lives of Aboriginal peoples. White Paper liberalism would
disband any hope of a workable theory of Aboriginal rights by 'justly
forcing' Aboriginal peoples to assimilate with the mainstream. The
White Paper served to rouse Aboriginal peoples from their colonial
slumbers and begin to question the legitimacy of liberal views of justice. The problem of Aboriginal participation began to take on a new
face after the ideas of the White Paper took hold in Indian Country.

Conclusion

In discussing the White Paper of 1969, I have shown that although the
paper was purporting to offer a more just vision of the Indian–white
political relationship, it was saying something very different to the
Indians of Canada. The White Paper claimed that the discriminatory

nature of the Indian–white relationship could be addressed by welcoming Indians into mainstream Canadian culture. By emphasizing that Indians are citizens, and therefore should not possess any special rights, the government could take practical steps to assimilate Indians into mainstream Canadian society.

Indians reacted strongly to this proposed (re)vision of the relationship. Harold Cardinal in *Unjust Society* spoke out angrily the content of the policy itself, declaring that Indians were still being ignored by the dominant culture and that Indian leaders were getting fed up with this kind of treatment. The inception of national organizations increased the Indian presence in Canadian politics. This was only at a 'consultative' level; even so, Indians began to play a larger role in shaping Indian politics at the national level. This culminated in the second part of the repatriated constitution, which embedded the rights of Aboriginal peoples in Canada's highest law.

A robust theory of Aboriginal rights is going to have to incorporate three central issues that White Paper liberalism failed to address: the legacy of colonialism; the idea that Aboriginal rights are group rights that flow out of Aboriginal peoples' status as indigenous nations (indigenous nationhood); and the concept that the existence of the Canadian state is not a given in the legal and political relationship. The only way these issues can be resolved in Canadian society is for Aboriginal peoples to participate more effectively in the practices that are followed to define their rights, sovereignty, and nationhood. I will soon explain in more detail the problem of Aboriginal participation in mainstream intellectual culture, but before I do, I will examine two prominent liberal theorists' responses to White Paper liberalism and discuss how their theories attempt to improve the legal and political status of Aboriginal peoples.

In the next two chapters I examine the work of Allan Cairns and Will Kymlicka, whose liberal theories address *some* of the White Paper's shortcomings but ultimately fail to incorporate Aboriginal participation into their theories of Aboriginal rights. They may believe they are offering more just alternatives to White Paper liberalism, but from an Aboriginal perspective, their understandings of Aboriginal rights continue to limit and thereby marginalize Aboriginal participation.

2 Cairns's Canada: Citizens Nonplussed

The imposition of uniformity does not lead to unity but to resistance, further repression and disunity. The proof is the dismal record in practice.

James Tully

If Alan Cairns is anything, he is an optimist. He believes wholeheartedly in the idea that Aboriginal and non-Aboriginal peoples can set aside their differences, whatever they are, and forge a renewed relationship based on the idea of shared citizenship. Cairns has been involved in, and written about, federal Canadian politics for almost forty years.[1] He has helped shape Canadian public policy and is well known for advocating the 'Citizens Plus' view, which he helped articulate in the Hawthorn Report of 1966.[2] In this chapter I argue that if we are to inject a form of indigenous nationhood into Canadian legal and political discourses and practices, Cairns's characterization of the political relationship is ultimately untenable. To show this, I divide this chapter into two sections.

In the first section, I examine Cairns's Citizens Plus view, focusing on two of his central ideas: the idea of shared citizenship and the distinction he makes between what he calls the 'assimilation' and 'parallel' policy paradigms in Canada.[3] Cairns argues that his view is a middle ground between the colonial policies of assimilation and unrealistic demands for a third order of government. I will show how the Citizens Plus view, though it considers Canada's colonial past, does not seriously address the issue of Aboriginal nationhood.[4] I argue that he fails to address the problem of Aboriginal participation and that his view is therefore unacceptable as a potential vision of a renewed political relationship between Aboriginal peoples and the Canadian state.

In the second section, I examine Cairns's understanding of the parallel model – in particular, his understanding of Iroquoian political thought and his use of the Two Row Wampum. Essentially, Cairns misinterprets the significance and meaning of the Two Row Wampum. This in turn casts doubts on the assimilation/parallel distinction he invokes to ground his supposedly more moderate position. When we examine the Two Row Wampum more closely – which calls for a brief consideration of early colonial Iroquoian political thought – we see that the Iroquois developed a sophisticated philosophy that Cairns fails to appreciate. Whether Iroquoian political thinking constitutes a parallel model or not, one thing is clear from Cairns's work: the Citizens Plus view remains committed to White Paper liberalism's idea that the sovereignty of the Canadian state is non-negotiable, and therefore would silence Aboriginal voices that defend various forms of indigenous nationhood.

Citizens Plus

Cairns's most recent book, *Citizens Plus*, is a reworking of the main ideas from the Hawthorn Report in the context of the post–section 35(1) era of Aboriginal rights. Cairns addresses one basic issue: 'The central question in Aboriginal/non-Aboriginal relations in Canada following European settlement has always been "Is the goal a single society with one basic model of belonging, or is the goal a kind of parallelism – a side by side coexistence – or some intermediate position?"'[5]

To answer this question, Cairns presents two models, which are supposed to represent two polarized extremes in Canada.[6] The first – the assimilation model – represents the politics of White Paper liberalism. There is no doubt that Cairns understands the importance of Canadian colonial history; he is sharply critical of the imperial attitudes that remain embedded in Canadian political practices. But he tempers much of his criticism of imperialism and colonialism by alluding to various 'facts' of the contemporary relationship. For example, throughout his book he expresses doubts about the feasibility of Aboriginal governance, noting that there has been a diaspora of Aboriginal peoples from the reserves into Canadian cities for decades, which makes the idea of self-government on treaty lands problematic. The government's program of assimilation, defended in the White Paper, is intended to make everyone equal citizens – by force if necessary. Furthermore, this model of citizenship represents an evolution in constitutional democratic thought and therefore is to be celebrated and held up a model of

contemporary democratic politics. Cairns does not want to do away
with Aboriginal rights – including some implementation of Aboriginal
self-government – but he defines such rights as authoritatively 'within'
the Canadian state.

The second model Cairns cites is (supposedly) assimilation's ideological opposite – the parallelism model, which emphasizes separateness and difference instead of sameness and equality. In the parallel
model, equality is emphasized at the group level, not at the individual
level. Individual rights still exist – the difference is that they do not
function as the sole normative force in a theory of justice. Cairns does
not explain the differences between the two models in the language of
justice; rather, he claims that the assimilationists emphasize sameness,
whereas parallel advocates emphasize difference. Cairns defends a
third option, which for him represents a middle ground: respect for
cultural differences between Aboriginal and non-Aboriginal people,
together with an emphasis on what they share politically. For Cairns,
this amounts to accepting that Aboriginal peoples were here first and
that the European newcomers through the course of the relationship
have failed to live up to their obligations. Aboriginal peoples, then, are
entitled to *some* form of special recognition, even though Canadian
citizenship is to be embraced equally by Aboriginal and non-Aboriginal
peoples.

Cairns contends, first and foremost, that the Citizens Plus approach is
a just response to the oppressive content of the White Paper. The White
Paper's advocacy of forced assimilation is no doubt fundamentally
unjust for Cairns. But he does not say *why* Aboriginal peoples have
legitimate claims against the state in the first place – what the source is
of the 'plus' in Citizens Plus – except to ascribe some moral legitimacy
to the claim that 'we were here first.' For example, the treaty federalism
position is quite clear: Aboriginal rights flow out of the fact that Aboriginal nations constitute legitimate political entities. Cairns never
engages the treaty federalists other than to say that Aboriginal peoples
have made the language of 'nation to nation' part of the political
relationship and that this kind of political victory cannot be ignored.
He believes that White Paper assimilation is wrong, but he does not
go on to admit that 'nation-to-nation' discourse is a move in the right
direction.

Cairns does not have to evaluate the indigenous nationhood position
because he limits the extent to which the state can recognize the legitimacy of Aboriginal nationhood:

The past treatment of Aboriginal peoples is neither a source of pride, nor a record of success. The elementary question that confronts us is which path do we follow in our search for a more fruitful relationship between Aboriginal and non-Aboriginal peoples in Canada. We do not have a clean slate. The momentum behind the drive to self-government and the support for the positive recognition of the Aboriginal presence in Canada are irresistible imperatives to which a wholehearted 'yes' is the only answer. *On the other hand*, the conditions that sustained the nation-to-nation relations of the early contact period have vanished. Our nation-to-nation relationship then was international. It is not so now and hence to so describe it even if only implicitly, without qualification, risks a damaging confusion.[7]

Cairns is not interested in providing the 'qualification' needed to justify the contemporary nation-to-nation relationship, because there is only one legitimate nation in the relationship, and that is Canada.

Imperialism and colonialism are realities in Canada, and we have inherited a legal and political system that has oppressed Aboriginal peoples. The first part of the Citizens Plus view unpacks the injustice of forced assimilation policies in Canada, with admonitions that this cannot be continued; the second part places limits on the actions the state should take to renew the relationship. The assimilation model has been a destructive force in Canadian politics, and we can no longer allow it to drive the Aboriginal-Canadian state relationship; but for Cairns, the renewed relationship, guided by the Citizens Plus model, unilaterally invokes its own imperatives.

First, the sovereignty of the Canadian state is a given, an absolute, and not up for negotiation in the political relationship. Cairns makes the point several times that Aboriginal peoples are unquestionably 'within' Canada. They can use the language of 'nationhood,' but in doing so they only add to the confusion because there is only one legitimate nation in the Aboriginal–Canadian state relationship: 'The future of Aboriginal peoples lies inside, not outside the Canadian state. Independence is not a realistically available option.'[8] In his conclusion he reiterates this point: 'The future of Aboriginal peoples, whether or not they have a land base that is a requisite for effective self-government, is within Canada. If that "withinness" means that Canada is to be more than a container, or a mini-international system, we need *bonds of empathy* so that our togetherness is moral as well as geographical.'[9]

The 'bonds of empathy' is an interesting choice of words, since they imply a moral dimension to the relationship. Presumably, these bonds are created by the interactions of citizens – all citizens – in society. It is difficult to see how this special bond is supposed to materialize, especially when oppressive policies such as the *Indian Act* continue to dictate the day-to-day lives of Aboriginal peoples.

Second, Cairns deems that because Aboriginal peoples are 'within' Canada, they are first and foremost citizens of the state. His view rests on the idea that Aboriginal peoples are unproblematically citizens of the state, and that despite colonial history and the oppressive nature of the contemporary relationship, they ought to see themselves mainly as full citizens of Canada. It is this 'fact' of the relationship that drives the Citizens Plus view. There are two problems with this claim. First, the statement is false. No doubt, many if not most Aboriginal people see themselves as Canadian citizens, but many see themselves as citizens of an indigenous nation *in addition* to (and often prior to) being citizens of Canada. In other words, Aboriginal political identities are multinational.[10] Second, that statement can be understood as true only if we ignore the colonial history of the political relationship, and in particular the significance of the treaty relationship. I will say more about this later.

The third imperative – which is a consequence of the previous claim – is that any recognition of Aboriginal rights in Canada will ultimately have to be articulated in the language of individual rights, and therefore amenable to the *Canadian Constitution*. This move accomplishes two things for Cairns. First, it makes a richer conception of Aboriginal nationhood impossible. Second, it makes the 'extra' rights that Aboriginal peoples possess individual rights, whose ultimate source is Aboriginal peoples' status as citizens of the state and not the fact that Aboriginal nations are legitimate political entities. This move proves to be very effective for Cairns, because if one looks at Aboriginal nationhood and the language of state sovereignty, it is difficult to accept that Aboriginal peoples can be citizens of the state *and* belong to recognized indigenous nations.

Allow me to summarize these three points of criticism:

1. The sovereignty of the Canadian state is absolute and not up for negotiation in the Aboriginal–Canadian state relationship. Cairns does not seriously consider that Aboriginal peoples may have claims against the state which predate the formation of the Canadian state. The legal problems associated with recognizing the

legitimacy of Aboriginal title in Canadian law, raised by McNeil and Borrows, do not arise for Cairns because the state is the ultimate source of political legitimacy. For Cairns, the discourse of nationhood is confusing, given that there is only one legitimate nation in the political relationship – the nation-state of Canada.

2. Because the sovereignty of the Canadian state is absolute, Aboriginal peoples are first and foremost citizens of the Canadian state. Cairns admits that Aboriginal peoples may belong to an Aboriginal 'nation,' and that this may entail the recognition of special rights; realistically, though, Canadian citizenship is the most important form of membership in the political relationship.

3. Because Aboriginal peoples are full citizens of the Canadian state, the special rights they possess are bestowed on them by the state, and the meaning of those special rights is articulated in the discourse of individual rights.

Clearly, when the sovereignty of the Canadian state is assumed to be absolute and non-negotiable, universal citizenship naturally follows. But how does the 'plus' in Citizens Plus arise for Cairns? His view is driven by the notion that Aboriginal peoples and other Canadians share the idea that they 'belong' to Canada. For Cairns, this translates into citizenship – Aboriginal peoples are citizens of Canada. Colonialism has tainted the relationship, but the idea of common citizenship mysteriously trumps Canada's colonial past. This is because, for Cairns, justice needs to be forward-looking, and common citizenship is a way for a nation to focus on the well-being of *everyone* while looking to a better shared future. But this means that colonialism, and the effects of colonialism, no longer play a central role in renewing the political relationship. For Cairns, colonialism amounts to a short list of remediable social and political problems, which can be solved by everyone looking forward and celebrating Canadian citizenship – as if what we share is enough to compel the government to find better solutions to Aboriginal problems.

The problem is, Cairns never provides a good reason why Aboriginal peoples ought to embrace Canadian citizenship as their *primary* source of political identity. Colonialism is not simply a laundry list of problems that can be overcome by the idea that common citizenship is enough to set the relationship on a just path of reconciliation. Reconciliation is not an idea that appeals to Cairns, although he agrees that the historical relationship has been oppressive and that the government should not be let off the hook. But Cairns does not see resolving the oppressive past as an insurmountable problem. Herein lies a central tension to Cairns's view. He believes we can bypass the problem of reconciliation because we have the power to clear the moral playing field. In other words, Canadians can renew the relationship, but not by seriously addressing what has gone wrong and rectifying it; rather, the relationship can be renewed by embracing a dialogical process that is driven by the sincere belief that all Canadians (including Aboriginal peoples) can find solutions guided by what they have in common. After all, Canadians and Aboriginal peoples share more than, say, Canadians and Russians.

But as Borrows and McNeil have pointed out, Aboriginal demands for justice question the legitimacy of the Canadian state's unilateral claim of sovereignty. Shared citizenship does not provide a rich enough framework to address the kinds of political problems Borrows and McNeil raise. So, Cairns sees Citizens Plus as a way of justly resolving unrealistic Aboriginal demands for self-government by asserting that Aboriginal issues have to be resolved 'within' Canada. Aboriginal people's own understandings of their rights, sovereignty, and nationhood are not constrained by the 'within Canada' imperative. Loosening Cairns from the 'within Canada' position is not going to be an easy task, as his understanding of Aboriginal nationhood does not have to pose a threat to Canadian unity. It will, however, require us to renew our conceptions of Canada – especially how Aboriginal peoples fit into the Canadian legal and political landscape.

There is another problem with Cairns's view. Adopting the ideological position of 'common' citizenship as a way of dealing with Aboriginal peoples is a colonial strategy. Although Cairns does not want to do away with history, he certainly wants to render competing historical interpretations irrelevant. His attitude towards incorporation is that for better or worse, Aboriginal people have been citizens of Canada. One historical interpretation he avoids is the Aboriginal interpretation of the treaties. For Aboriginal peoples, the treaties have a normative role in the contemporary relationship because they recognize rights that Aboriginal peoples possess by virtue of their unique political status, not by virtue of a shared citizenship. In other words, for many Aboriginal people Aboriginal rights are political rights that predate the formation of the Canadian state, not rights that arise from a post-Confederation concept of shared citizenship.

A way to summarize what I have been saying about the Citizens Plus view is that many Aboriginal people simply do not share Cairns's idea of shared citizenship. But there are other, I think deeper, problems with the Citizens Plus view. Cairns characterizes the Two Row Wampum as a parallel form of governance. I will show in the next section he misunderstands Iroquoian political thinking.

Indigenous Parallelism – The *Guswentha* as Political Philosophy

Cairns cites the Iroquoian *Guswentha*, or 'Two Row Wampum,' as an example of a parallel view of the political relationship that ultimately is untenable. Cairns states:

> The two-row wampum model so frequently proposed as the arrangement that will fit our needs, stresses the permanence of difference. As an image it postulates parallel paths that never converge. The image is coexistence with little traffic between the solitudes. It does not suggest shared endeavours for a common purpose. Further, of course, parallelism has little to offer the growing urban Aboriginal population, jumbled up with other Canadians. Its vision is of distinct peoples coexisting in a side-by-side relationship – friendly, perhaps, but with little appetite for common endeavours. Parallelism – the two-row wampum – does not address the reality of our interdependence, and of our intermingling. It speaks, therefore, to only part of who we are.[11]

What is remarkable about Cairns's use of what I will call 'two row' political thinking is that he fails to understand or appreciate the depth of Iroquoian philosophical thought. In doing so, he caricatures Iroquoian political thinking, which in turn affects the way we ought to understand his Citizens Plus view. Before returning to Cairns's use (or misuse) of the Guswentha in his Citizens Plus view, it is important that we contextualize the Guswentha as an exemplar of indigenous political thinking.

One of the fundamental differences between European and indigenous cultures is that indigenous peoples have a highly developed oral tradition. Oral traditions are very much alive in most indigenous communities, and it is only recently that indigenous peoples have engaged the written word. N. Scott Momaday, a Kiowa writer, captures the importance of words, and promises, for indigenous cultures in his book *The Way to Rainy Mountain*:

A word has power in and of itself. It comes from nothing into sound and meaning; it gives origin to all things. By means of words can a man deal with the world on equal terms. And the word is sacred. A man's name is his own; he can keep it or give it away as he likes.

For example, consider the following story:

If an arrow is well made, it will have tooth marks upon it. That is how you know. The Kiowas made fine arrows and straightened them in their teeth. Then they drew them to the bow to see if they were straight. Once there was a man and his wife. They were alone at night in their tipi. By the light of the fire the man was making arrows. After a while he caught sight of something. There was a small opening in the tipi where the two hides were sewn together. Someone was there on the outside looking in. The man went on with his work, but he said to his wife: 'Someone is standing outside. Do not be afraid. Let us talk easily, as of ordinary things.' He took up the arrow and straightened it in his teeth; then as it was right for him to do, he drew it to the bow and took aim, first in this direction and that. And all the while he was talking, as if to his wife. But this is how he spoke: 'I know that you are there on the outside, for I can feel your eyes upon me. If you are a Kiowa, you will understand what I am saying, and you will speak your name.' But there was no answer, and the man went on in the same way, pointing the arrow all around. At last his aim fell upon the place where his enemy stood, and he let go of the string. The arrow went straight to the enemy's heart.[12]

This old story is still important for the Kiowa, and for indigenous peoples: we need to ask how language can help us survive in the contemporary world. The first quote illustrates that for many indigenous peoples, possessing power over one's language is a sacred capacity. Perhaps the social and political realities have changed drastically since the early days of contact; even so, indigenous strategies for engaging philosophical problems through the oral tradition remain an essential part of indigenous identity. The story of the arrow maker is a profound lesson in the importance of language and belonging and shows how one's language is often a necessary means of survival. Indigenous peoples have long been aware of the importance of language and of preserving it against the onslaught of colonialism. But language does more than secure a sense of belonging; it also provides the philosophical framework for indigenous ways of knowing the world.

And for most indigenous cultures, these ways of knowing are embodied in the oral tradition.

In contrast, philosophical discourse in the European tradition, has evolved around the legitimacy of the 'text.' Philosophy is written, published, and consumed within a literate, mostly university-educated community of practitioners. The written text plays a central role in determining what counts as legitimate content in philosophical discourse. A defining characteristic of the text in Western philosophy is that it focuses on presenting coherent and developed arguments. Philosophers defend arguments, which consist of premises and conclusions, which are evaluated against a set of standards that have evolved in the course of the European philosophical tradition. This is a very brief outline of this philosophical tradition; my point is that for the European philosophical community, the written text is the main form of philosophical discourse, whereas indigenous philosophy is rooted in oral traditions.[13]

Iroquoian peoples in early colonial America were well known for their highly developed rules of diplomacy, which focused on the importance of oratory.[14] An oral account, be it a speech or a narrative, was given in a particular context – for example, a treaty negotiation. Once agreement was reached among the participating parties, wampum belts were exchanged. Wampum are small shells that are bored through the middle and strung into belts or strings. Wampum had many meanings, each depending on the context. The main political significance of wampum was to represent – materially – the morally binding nature of an agreement or promise. This was a way of sanctifying one's words in practice. Wampum belts served as the 'text' in the sense that they materialized the agreement itself. What made the wampum belts valuable was that each had a story attached to it that certain people, called wampum keepers, were responsible for remembering and reciting at various times of the year. The physical act of giving or receiving the wampum belt established the moral significance of the agreement.[15]

Wampum belts were exchanged in the context of reciprocity and renewal – two central concepts in Iroquoian political thought – which meant that the normative terms of a political agreement were renewed in a context of peace, respect, and friendship. Issues of interpretation and of determining the meaning of particular treaties, then, were not so much a philosophical problem as a practical problem. Treaties, such as the early friendship treaties, required constant renewal, and agreements could only be made with the consent of both sides. If one side did not agree, there would be no exchange of wampum belts. If the two sides could not reach an agreement, often they would go to war. Of course, interpreting the meaning of particular wampum belts was not possible without an understanding of the social and political context from which they arose; but this does not mean they were closed to philosophical interpretation.[16]

The Guswentha is an example of an Iroquoian treaty that embraces a profound political vision. There is some controversy over the origins of the Guswentha, but many Iroquoians claim that it originated early in the relationship with the Europeans and was first exchanged with the Dutch. Grand Chief Michael Mitchell of Akwesasne states, and he is worth quoting in full:

> When the Haudenosaunee first came into contact with the European nations, treaties of peace and friendship were made. Each was symbolized by the Gus-Wen-Teh or Two Row Wampum. There is a bed of white wampum which symbolizes the purity of the agreement. There are two rows of purple, and those rows have the spirit of your ancestors and mine. There are three beads of wampum separating the two rows and they symbolize peace, friendship and respect.
>
> These two rows symbolize two paths or vessels, traveling down the same rivers together. One, a birch bark canoe, will be for the Indian people, their laws, their customs and their ways. The other, a ship, will be for the white people and their laws, their customs and their ways. We shall each travel the river together, side by side, but in our own boat. Neither of us will try to steer the other's vessel.
>
> The principles of the Two Row Wampum became the basis for all treaties and agreements that were made with the Europeans and later the Americans.[17]

It is crucial to point out that Cairns fails to mention that there are three beads, representing peace, respect, and friendship, that bridge the two parallel rows. This is a serious oversight because understanding the meaning and significance of these three beads helps explain what the Iroquois mean by a just political relationship.[18]

The Grand Council, which was organized from the Confederacy, was not a European type of centralized government. Representation within the Grand Council consisted of fifty chiefs, or sachems, who represented the voices of their communities. The chiefs did not make decisions in consultation with other chiefs about the welfare of the community as a whole without *first* gaining the approval of their respective communities. This process was respected for every issue that affected the welfare of the Confederacy. This kind of democratic representation was grounded in the principles of reciprocity and renewal. These two fundamental principles are deeply embedded in Iroquois culture, and they generate attitudes that guide social and political relationships at all levels of interaction. These principles are pivotal to understanding the Iroquois notion of political sovereignty and are worth a closer examination.

According to the Great Law of Peace, a human being possesses intrinsic value and ought to be accorded respect.[19] The notion of respect goes to the core of Iroquoian religious thought; but in a political context, respecting another person's intrinsic value means that you recognize that they have the right to speak their mind and to choose for themselves how to act in the world. It follows that in principle, one cannot tell another what to do or how to behave. Europeans often commented on the individualistic nature of Native Americans and on the fundamental respect and freedom they accorded one another in their daily lives.[20]

But respect functioned in a communal context; that is, individual respect was reciprocated. This form of reciprocity is what gave rise to freedom of speech and freedom of religion. In many indigenous communities it was considered disrespectful to speak for another, and it was certainly forbidden to choose for another how to act. The freedom of speech gave everyone the right to speak his or her mind, but it was embedded in the context that everyone else possessed the same right.

It is also important to note that reciprocity applied to groups as well as to individuals. Longhouses and nations were recognized as autonomous entities, and thus were accorded rights to govern themselves as they saw fit. This recognition, however, had its limits, for reciprocity and self-government were only fully recognized *after* one embraced the Great Peace. I will come back to this limitation shortly, when I discuss the notion of political power.

Religious (or spiritual) diversity was a fact duly recognized by virtually every Iroquoian, and the Confederacy accommodated this diversity in its political structure. However, Iroquoians – like many indigenous peoples – share an implicit assumption that there is a supreme Creator. Cosmologically, this Creator created the universe and is responsible for sustaining its natural order. Ceremonies are a natural part of religion as they are ways to give thanks to the Creator and to confirm one's place in the universe. Given the praxis of reciprocity, it follows that people give thanks in different ways and therefore embrace different ceremonies and religions. When the Europeans arrived, their beliefs were no less respected than other existing Native American religions. As is well documented, the European missionaries did not hold the same view of reciprocity. A fundamental difference between European and Native American political thinking related to how each recognized the diversity of religious beliefs within a political community.[21] The Iroquoian attitude of reciprocity was tightly woven into yet another culturally embedded principle, that of renewal.

The concept of renewal is complex; along with respect and reciprocity, it goes to the core of Iroquoian political philosophy. The main idea behind the principle of renewal is that change is a natural part of any relationship whether that relationship is spiritual, physical, or political. This is because nature moves in cycles of renewal: life and death; the four seasons; planting cycles; migration patterns, and so on.[22] Relationships between people go through natural changes as well. For the Iroquois it is important to periodically recognize, affirm, and renew a relationship in order to revitalize it so that peaceful coexistence can be preserved. Public manifestations of the principles of reciprocity and renewal are found in the various forms of the Condolence Ceremony.

Renewal in political relationships, though, depends on an important proviso of the Condolence Ceremony – that keeping one's word within the public sphere is recognized by everyone to be of utmost importance in securing and maintaining peace.[23] Promises made in the public domain are elevated to the highest standards of diplomatic protocol. Of course, there are no guarantees that everyone will tell the truth, so even in diplomatic situations one is never 'sure' the truth is being told. The indigenous approach to resolving this unavoidable human problem is to sanctify certain practices. Words are to be used in responsible ways, and in certain situations they bind a person to keep a promise. This was especially true if there had been an exchange of wampum. But the place of oral agreements must be understood in the context of a culture based on an oral tradition.

Another example of a 'text' in indigenous oral traditions is what has come to be known as the 'narrative.' For example, the life of The Peacemaker is an indigenous narrative. This narrative was originally spoken, not read. But for indigenous peoples, narratives function in the context of respect, reciprocity, and renewal. For example, a story would be recited to children and it would be up to the children themselves to think about the story. They could confer with other people, especially elders, about its meaning and significance, but each child had to reach an understanding of its meaning on his or her own. Narratives, or stories, do 'contain' messages and morals, but they are offered to listeners in ways that allow the listener to decide for himself or herself what the story means and whether it carries an important moral lesson. Because stories are retold many times, and by different people, a kind of communal moral landscape develops, and by participating in this landscape a community develops a shared conception of morality.

Since the latter half of the nineteenth century, non-indigenous anthropologists and missionaries have been transcribing indigenous narratives into written texts. This means that texts of indigenous narratives are now available for academic scrutiny.[24] Once the European newcomers gained a political advantage over the Iroquois, the wampum belts ceased to be recognized as legitimate sources for understanding the significance and meaning of the treaties. An important fact that is often overlooked is that the oral tradition remains alive in many indigenous communities and has evolved to embrace the written text.[25] There can be no doubt that in many contemporary contexts, especially legal and political contexts, the written text has taken primacy over oral accounts. However, in early contact the Iroquois *and* the Europeans considered the oral tradition not only a legitimate way to understand treaties but also the source of Iroquoian knowledge and wisdom.[26]

One important consequence of the primacy of an oral tradition is that words, metaphors, and symbols play a major role in determining social and political meanings, especially in the context of 'indigenous politics.' 'The basic principle of Iroquois metaphor is the projection of words about familiar objects and relations onto the fields of politics and diplomacy.'[27] Metaphors are used in many cultures to guide political relationships, but one has to be especially careful about the use of metaphors in Iroquoian political thought. Certain Iroquoian metaphors – of which I shall discuss two – do not easily translate into European equivalents.

First, there is the importance of kinship metaphors. The use of familial terms in Iroquoian diplomacy established power relations between the participating parties. The relationship between father and children is not the same in Iroquoian culture as in European families: in Iroquoian culture the father does not carry significant paternal authority over his children. Iroquoian societies are matrilineal, which means that the eldest matriarch possesses the ultimate moral and political authority within each clan. The uncles on the mother's side are viewed as having authority over the children. Grandfathers are deeply respected, but they do not command obedience. The title of 'brother' or 'brethren' demands a relationship of equality, although a distinction is made between elder and younger brother that dictates a protocol of deference in speaking, as is found in the protocol of Grand Council meetings. With regard to the European–Iroquoian political relationship, the Iroquois always considered Europeans their brethren. When the Europeans insisted on being addressed as 'father,' Iroquoians did so to enable further negotiations and to create certain obligations on the part of the Europeans, not because they saw themselves as children of the king of France in a European sense.[28] For the Iroquois, the relevant political relationship of equality was between brothers; it was not the paternal relationship dictated by early Europeans.

The second metaphor involves the sanctity of words. I have already discussed the importance of words in the context of treaties, but it is important to reiterate the point. Words, as expressed in promises or political agreements, become morally binding when they are accompanied by the exchange of wampum or the smoking of the pipe. The wampum belts played a central role in securing a respectful political relationship in Iroquoia. Sometimes a wampum belt was given as a gift to confirm one's position in a particular relationship.[29]

Tobacco is a sacred plant for virtually all indigenous peoples. In a political context, smoking the pipe represents the solemnity of taking responsibility for one's words. In diplomatic relationships, the act of smoking the pipe represents carrying one's words with the smoke into the spirit world. In many indigenous world views, the spirit world is the highest form of existence as it is the place where ancestors went when they died. To breach the sanctity of this act is a fundamental expression of disrespect that upsets the balance of peace in the political relationship. Father Marquette says in the *Jesuit Relations* that the sacred pipe 'is the most mysterious thing in the World. The Scepters of our Kings are not as much respected; for the Savages have such a Deference for this Pipe, that one may call it the God of Peace and War, and the Arbiter of Life and Death.'[30]

Smoking the pipe, then, morally binds the participants in a solemn manner, and does so in a way that requires them to take responsibility for themselves. Political agreements were publicly legitimized *because* they were consecrated in the pipe ceremony. Compare this indigenous practice to the practice where 'signed and sealed articles of agreement ... were most often considered by Euroamericans to be the primary concrete symbols of agreement, [although they] were not commonly valued as such by Iroquois people.'[31]

To complicate matters, it was never certain that both sides fully understood what the political agreements meant. This is why the notion of power is central to understanding the political structure of the Iroquois Confederacy. For example, The Peacemaker's message of Righteousness and Power states: 'Righteousness means justice practiced between men and between nations; it means also a desire to see justice prevail. Power means authority, the authority of law and custom, backed by such force as is necessary to make justice prevail; it means also religion, for justice enforced is the will of the Holder of the Heavens and has his sanction.'[32]

An Iroquoian conception of justice centres on the idea that all people can live in peaceful coexistence provided they respect the moral autonomy of the other. There are several assumptions at work in this view of justice. Besides the principles of respect, reciprocity, and renewal mentioned above, another Iroquoian assumption about human nature is that rational human beings, or those of 'good mind,' desire peace rather than disorder and war.[33]

For the Iroquois, justice has to be put to use in the everyday world; that is, a just society is not something that happens on its own. This is where the principle of renewal returns to our discussion. Political relationships require renewing – if they are left alone they die. Political relationships, by their very meaning, cannot escape the problem of power. Throughout the sixteenth and seventeenth centuries, the Five Nations had the physical power to enforce their will in and around Iroquoia. However, the military force exercised by the Confederacy was only used if necessary to situate a community within the Confederacy. Once a community embraced the Great Law of Peace, it could govern itself as it saw fit, as long as it did not infringe on the other nations in the Confederacy. Parker says: 'Whenever a foreign nation is conquered or has by its own free will accepted the Great Peace, their own system of internal government may continue so far as is consistent but they shall cease all strife with other nations.'[34]

Another characterization of the Great Law of Peace offers the image of a great tree:

[The Peacemaker's] tree had four white roots that stretched to the four directions of the earth. A snow white carpet of thistledown spread out from the base of the tree, covering the surrounding countryside and protecting the peoples who embraced the three life affirming principles. [The Peacemaker] explained that this tree was humanity, living within the principles governing relations among human beings, and the eagle perched on top of the giant pine was humanity's lookout against enemies who would disturb the peace. He postulated that the white carpet could cover the entire earth and provide a shelter of peace and brotherhood for all mankind. His vision was a message from the Creator, bringing harmony to human existence and uniting all peoples into a single family.[35]

So one had to become a member of the political community – by force if necessary – in order to exercise its privileges.[36] Democracy had its price in the Confederacy: one had to accept the Great Law of Peace before one could be recognized as belonging to the Confederacy. Perhaps this 'forcing one to be free' provision worked in early colonial Iroquoia because the Iroquois were a strong military force at the time and did not hesitate to use their physical superiority whenever they thought it was in their best interests; however, political power functioned in a way that was quite different from European governments. To explain why, I return to the Guswentha.

The Guswentha is guided by the Great Law of Peace, which embraces several deeply embedded principles of behaviour. The principles of respect, reciprocity, and renewal are central to Iroquoian political thinking, especially when we attempt to understand how political relationships are maintained in practice. These principles make sense of the relationship between the two purple rows: the two participants in the political relationship – Europeans and Iroquois – can share the same space and travel into the future, yet neither can steer the other's vessel. Because they share the same space, they are inextricably entwined in a relationship of interdependence – *but they remain distinct political entities.* Cairns fails to understand this because he omits an important part of the political relationship: the three beads of respect, peace, and friendship that bind the two rows together *but as independent nations.* Respect, peace, and friendship are pivotal to *maintaining* the relationship, not to establishing it. These principles need to be renewed if they are to function properly: healthy political relationships are dynamic, and the participants need to have certain attitudes if the relationships are to evolve in a respectful and peaceful environment.

Yet another dimension to Iroquoian political thinking is worth mentioning. One reason why the Two Row Wampum is useful for a kind of 'pan-indigenous' political thinking is that it demonstrates that Euro-

pean nations became nations because of the forms of political recognition the Iroquois *bestowed* on them. The kind of nationhood that remains
embedded in Iroquoia has retained its normative force throughout the
historical relationship. This supports McNeil and Borrows's thesis that
the Canadian legal system has gained its legitimacy by virtue of indigenous law.

This brief diversion into Iroquoian political thought is not so much
about laying out an Iroquoian political world view – that would be like
trying to explain Hegel on one page. My aim is to show that Iroquoian
political thought is complex, systematic, and philosophical. That Cairns
does not appreciate this is reflected in his attitude towards the Two Row
Wampum. I am not arguing that the Two Row is *the* best way to
understand the meaning of Aboriginal rights in Canada. I am making a
much simpler point: I am suggesting that Cairns fails to listen to indigenous ways of understanding politics when he incorporates indigenous
peoples into his view of justice. In addition, his assumption about the
supremacy of Canadian sovereignty implies that the concept of indigenous nationhood is not required in his discussion of Aboriginal rights.
By invoking the unilateral assertion of Canadian sovereignty, and its
concomitant proviso that any form of Aboriginal self-government will
have to be 'within' Canada, he is ignoring what many Aboriginal peoples
are asserting about the nature of the political relationship. Instead of
engaging in a difficult moral and political dialogue with Aboriginal
peoples, he is unilaterally setting down limits for *any* political dialogue
to occur, and justifying these limits by appealing to the colonial assumptions that have maintained the status quo.

The meaning of 'within' Canada is itself up for negotiation precisely
because it is a contested concept in the political relationship. Cairns does
away with any possible discussion by invoking what he takes to be a
practical constraint – self-government will be limited, and if it is recognized at all, it will be adjudicated within Canadian legal and political
practices. Many Aboriginal peoples do not question that they are Canadian, but it does not follow that they embrace Cairns's view of citizenship. Cairns does not want to embrace the treaty federalism route, but
many Aboriginal peoples do. Does this point of disagreement constitute
a philosophical problem? I believe it does, and I will discuss the problem in greater detail in chapter 5. Can Cairns's view accommodate such
a disagreement? Not in its present form, as the problem of Aboriginal
participation remains unresolved. This is why I cannot embrace his way
of understanding Aboriginal rights.

3 Liberalism's Last Stand: Minority Rights and the (Mis)recognition of Aboriginal Sovereignty

Whatever else he denounces in our culture he is certain that it still possesses the moral resources which he requires in order to denounce it. Everything else may be, in his eyes, in disorder; but the language of morality is in order, just as it is. That he too may be being betrayed by the very language he uses is not a thought available to him.

Alasdair MacIntyre

Aboriginal rights, as they are entrenched in Canada's *Constitution Act, 1982*, can be interpreted as rights that are accorded to Aboriginal peoples by virtue of their membership in minority cultures.[1] This characterization of Aboriginal rights, derived from various styles of liberalism, does not recognize the legitimacy of indigenous forms of political sovereignty. Sovereignty does not play an important role in determining the content of Aboriginal special rights because within the framework of liberal thought, it simply does not exist.[2] As we have seen, Cairns's Citizens Plus view accords legitimate political sovereignty only to the provincial and federal governments. Aboriginal rights, then, if they exist at all, are subsumed within the superior forms of sovereignty held by the provincial and federal governments.

In this chapter I examine what many consider a generous account of Aboriginal rights and raise several serious concerns about this liberal characterization of Aboriginal rights. Since most Aboriginal communities claim that their 'special' rights flow from their legitimate political sovereignty,[3] I take issue with liberal claims that Aboriginal rights imply a type of 'minority right.' I then suggest why most Aboriginal peoples do not subscribe to liberalism's descriptions of their rights as minority rights. In view of Aboriginal understandings of their political sovereignty, justice demands that contemporary and future policy makers include Aboriginal voices when drafting legislation and policies that affect the welfare of Aboriginal peoples. In other words, a robust account of Aboriginal rights must include greater Aboriginal participation.

From an Aboriginal perspective, it is unfortunate that an investigation into the meaning of Aboriginal sovereignty must begin with an examination of liberalism. This is necessary because Aboriginal conceptions of sovereignty are not fully recognized as legitimate by Canada's federal and provincial governments. As Will Kymlicka states in *Liberalism, Community, and Culture*:

> For better or worse, it is predominantly non-Aboriginal judges and politicians who have the ultimate power to protect and enforce Aboriginal rights, and so it is important to find a justification of them that such people can recognize and understand. Aboriginal people have their own understanding of self-government drawn from their own experience, and that is important. But it is also important, politically, to know how non-Aboriginal Canadians – Supreme Court Justices, for example – will understand Aboriginal rights and relate them to their own experiences and traditions ... On the standard interpretation of liberalism, Aboriginal rights are viewed as matters of discrimination and/or privilege, not of equality. They will always, therefore, be viewed with the kind of suspicion that led liberals like Trudeau to advocate their abolition. Aboriginal rights, at least in their robust form, will only be secure when they are viewed, not as competing with liberalism, but as an essential component of liberal political practice.[4]

This imperative, which I refer to as 'Kymlicka's constraint,' represents a profound reality check for Aboriginal peoples. I agree with Kymlicka that Aboriginal rights 'in their robust form' ought not to compete with liberalism. But it is not simply a matter of waking liberals from their colonial slumbers in order to show them that Aboriginal forms of sovereignty make sense in the language of political liberalism. Indigenous peoples have tried for more than five hundred years to make colonial governments recognize the legitimacy of indigenous forms of political sovereignty.

I will use Kymlicka's classification of Aboriginal rights of governance as a special class of minority rights in order to show that his theory of minority rights requires us to include, and recognize, Aboriginal explanations of political sovereignty. So in one sense, I am contributing to the rich tradition of Aboriginal voices that have argued in favour of Aboriginal sovereignty. I differ from my predecessors in that I am not justifying or generating a theory of Aboriginal sovereignty at all; rather, I am going to engage Kymlicka's version of liberalism and show that it is not tenable *unless* it recognizes Aboriginal understandings of political sovereignty.

But my goals are not solely philosophical. I believe that Aboriginal conceptions of political sovereignty must be included in political liberalism's justification of Aboriginal rights so that the racist and oppressive public policies that have held Aboriginal peoples captive for more than one hundred thirty years can be changed. One way of renewing a just relationship – and more importantly, renewing hope among Aboriginal peoples – is to help non-Aboriginal peoples understand better the meaning and significance of Aboriginal forms of political sovereignty. The precise content of a theory of Aboriginal sovereignty will remain open, as indeed it should; the meaning of Aboriginal sovereignty in all its diversity is best understood by listening to the myriad voices of Aboriginal peoples themselves.

My discussion will fall into two sections. In the first, I briefly discuss Kymlicka's liberal theory of minority rights. For Kymlicka, Aboriginal rights are a special class of rights within a general theory of minority rights. He argues that Aboriginal rights do not pose a problem for liberalism, since they can be subsumed within a more general liberal theory of rights. Arguably, his liberalism offers the most generous accommodation of Aboriginal rights in contemporary liberalism; in fact, he is a strong advocate of Aboriginal self-government.

In the second section, I examine more closely Kymlicka's characterization of Aboriginal communities as 'national minorities' that somehow became 'incorporated' into the Canadian state. Kymlicka himself points out that this notion of incorporation is problematic and fraught with historical injustice. I will emphasize that a thorough understanding of 'Aboriginal incorporation' (my own term) goes to the heart of our understandings of Aboriginal sovereignty and especially of how we ought to understand the historical relationship between Aboriginal peoples and the European newcomers.

In the limited space of this chapter – indeed, of this book – I cannot provide a fully developed 'theory' of Aboriginal forms of political sovereignty. I do, however, have room to suggest what I consider a more fruitful way of approaching this complex issue without necessarily discarding Kymlicka's liberalism. Essentially, in this chapter, I take up Kymlicka's idea of Aboriginal incorporation to show that a thorough investigation of the meaning of this concept requires a radical shift in our understandings of historical interpretation, political sovereignty, and most importantly, Aboriginal peoples' place in the Canadian state.

Kymlicka on the Liberal Theory of Minority Rights[5]

Kymlicka begins *Liberalism, Community, and Culture* by stating that he will be examining the 'broader account of the relationship between the individual and society.'[6] In other words, he is interested in the individual's sense of belonging to a community and, therefore, to a culture. He proposes to defend an interpretation of liberalism – one influenced by Rawls and Dworkin – against communitarian objections that it possesses only a 'thin' theory of culture.[7] Communitarians mean by this objection that contemporary liberal theorists attach little value to the role culture plays in shaping an individual's moral and political identity. Supposedly, contemporary liberalism is unable to generate a rich or 'thick' theory of culture, given the diversity of cultures prevalent in most constitutional democracies.[8] There are two facets to the liberal–communitarian debate that Kymlicka wants to examine: the communitarian critiques demanding thick theories of culture, and the failure of both liberals and communitarians to deal with cultural diversity.

Kymlicka focuses on liberalism as a normative political philosophy, and examines what he takes to be the fundamental moral commitments made by a liberal political theory. The philosophical issue at hand is this: How is an individual to determine what her essential interest is when she deliberates about her moral status in the world? For Kymlicka, our essential interest is the fact that we attempt to live a good life; that is, we value most those things a good life contains. However, the current set of beliefs we hold to be of greatest value may be the wrong ones. So it is imperative that we be able to deliberate so that we can change our minds (when we come to consider certain beliefs that we have held to be inimical to the good life). Thus for Kymlicka our essential interest is living *the* good life – as opposed to the life we currently believe to be good.[9] Next, according to Kymlicka, we must revise these beliefs from 'the inside.' An individual can lead a good life only if she makes choices according to the values she holds to be true. Kymlicka has two preconditions for what he takes to be the necessary conditions for the fulfilment of our essential interest in leading a good life. First, we must lead our life from the inside – that is, from the set of beliefs we value as the best for our pursuit of the good life. Second, we must be free to question these beliefs.[10]

Kymlicka introduces culture into his theory because we must evaluate our beliefs in a cultural context. In his earlier book *Liberalism, Community, and Culture,* he does not offer a substantive understanding of culture, because he is not interested in exploring culture per se, but rather in establishing a set of rationally devised cultural conditions: 'Individuals must have the cultural *conditions* conducive to acquiring an awareness of different views of the good life, and to acquiring the ability to intelligently examine and reexamine these views.'[11] These cultural conditions must allow individuals to live their lives from the inside; furthermore, these individuals must have the freedom to question their beliefs in 'the light of whatever information and examples and arguments our culture can provide.' The culture Kymlicka is referring to as 'ours' has shown great concern for the rights of individuals. The liberal's explicit interest in the individual has forged the traditional liberal concerns for (Kymlicka's list) 'education, freedom of expression, freedom of press, artistic freedom, etc.'[12]

Kymlicka offers a more substantive discussion of culture in *Multicultural Citizenship: A Liberal Theory of Minority Rights*: 'The sort of culture that I will focus on is a *societal culture* – that is, a culture which provides its members with meaningful ways of life across the full range of human activities, including social, educational, religious, recreational, and economic life, encompassing both public and private spheres. These cultures tend to be territorially concentrated, and based on a shared language.'[13]

Moreover, a societal culture is 'institutionally' embodied. Clearly, Kymlicka has the same type of community in mind here as he offered in *Liberalism, Community, and Culture*; specifically, a legitimate societal culture is 'modern' and shares a common identity with an underlying commitment to individual equality and opportunity.[14] The public policies of this type of societal culture are guided by three imperatives: first, the government must treat people as equals; second, the government must treat all individuals with equal concern and respect; and third, the government must provide all individuals with the appropriate liberties and resources they need to examine and act on their beliefs. These criteria constitute a liberal conception of justice. So for Kymlicka, it is vital for an individual to choose what is best for the good life and to be free to act on these choices: 'For meaningful individual choice to be possible, individuals need not only access to information, the capacity to reflectively evaluate it, and freedom of expression and association. They also need access to a societal culture. Group-differentiated measures that secure and promote this access may, therefore, have a legitimate role to play in a liberal theory of justice.'[15]

Cultural membership, then, is a primary good in Kymlicka's liberalism.[16] Because culture is a primary good for all individuals, governments ought to preserve the integrity of the plurality of cultures from which individuals make their choices. Kymlicka identifies 'two broad patterns of cultural diversity.' In the first instance, 'cultural diversity arises from the *incorporation* of *previously* self-governing, territorially concentrated cultures into a larger state. These incorporated cultures, which I call "national minorities," typically wish to maintain themselves as distinct societies alongside the majority culture, and demand various forms of autonomy or self-government to ensure their survival as distinct societies.'[17]

The second pattern of cultural diversity arises out of 'individual and familial immigration.' Essentially, immigrants came to Canada under the assumption that they were going to become part of the existing societal culture; in a sense, they left behind their own societal cultures in order to join another. One of the main arguments of *Multicultural Citizenship* is that national minorities have stronger claims to group-differentiated rights than cultures that have immigrated to Canada from other parts of the world. In the Canadian context, the national minorities consist of the English and Scottish newcomers, the French newcomers, and the Aboriginal peoples.

Kymlicka claims that national minorities, as *previously* self-governing cultures, *incorporated* to form the Canadian state. He adds: 'The incorporation of different nations into a single state may be involuntary, as occurs when one cultural community is invaded and conquered by another, or is ceded from one imperial power to another, or when its homeland is overrun by colonizing settlers.'[18]

From an Aboriginal perspective, the Canadian state came into existence through all three practices: some Aboriginal communities were conquered,[19] some communities ceded powers to the British Crown and later to the Canadian governments, and many communities were simply overrun by colonial newcomers. Of course, these three practices were not exclusive to one another; most Aboriginal communities experienced all three forms of incorporation. I will return to the issue of

Aboriginal incorporation later; first I will take a closer look at Kymlicka's justification for the special rights held by national minorities.

In chapter 6 of *Multicultural Citizenship*, 'Justice and Minority Rights,' Kymlicka provides several overlapping arguments to justify minority rights, or group-differentiated rights, within a liberal democratic state. He discusses three arguments in favour of recognizing minority rights: the equality argument, the argument from historical agreement, and the diversity argument. As we will see shortly, his theory is driven by the equality argument; the historical agreement and diversity arguments, although meritorious on their own, ultimately depend on the equality argument for normative support.

Kymlicka's main motive in providing three overlapping justifications for minority rights is to show that the concept of 'benign neglect' is untenable for political liberalism. Advocates of the benign neglect view argue that recognition of universal individual rights resolves any problems associated with demands for special cultural recognition – according to this view, substantive differences between cultures are unproblematic because the state grants the same package of rights to all individuals. For their part, advocates of group-differentiated rights contend that there are substantive differences between the diverse cultures and that legitimate recognition of this diversity requires the state to allocate different packages of rights accordingly. Kymlicka argues that 'the state unavoidably promotes certain cultural identities, and thereby disadvantages others. Once we recognize this, we need to re-think the justice of minority rights claims.'[20] The equality argument is intended to resolve the conflict between the benign neglect view of rights and the group-differentiated rights view.[21]

The normative role of equality, in Kymlicka's equality argument, now functions at the level of the national minorities. Since cultural membership is a primary good *and* Aboriginal peoples constitute a national minority, those peoples are accorded special rights by the state – where the state is implicitly understood as *the* ultimate legitimate expression of political sovereignty. Aboriginal rights are a legitimate class of rights since liberals give credence to the intuition that prior occupancy has at least some normative weight in a theory of justice; indeed, in Kymlicka's theory this intuition is what generates the legitimacy of national minorities.[22] The special rights that Aboriginal peoples possess are rights of governance, one of three forms of group-differentiated rights in Kymlicka's theory of minority rights. These rights – the inherent rights that are legitimate from the initial formation of the

Canadian state – are the strongest form of group rights in Kymlicka's classification of minority rights. The other forms of group-differentiated rights – ethnic rights and special representation rights – are allocated to certain groups that arrived after the Canadian state was formed and do not entail rights of governance.[23]

Kymlicka's equality argument can be summarized as follows. The national minorities (Aboriginal peoples, the English, and the French) are the fundamentally privileged sovereign groups in Kymlicka's characterization of the Canadian multinational state. National minorities have rights of governance because they were the initial legitimate entities that formed the multinational state of Canada. However, for various reasons, the national minorities relinquished or transferred certain powers to the larger political union. Kymlicka notes that the creation of the multinational state may not have arisen from a just context; however, this poses no significant problem for his theory because his view of the political relationship *today* is premised on the fundamental political recognition of equality between the incorporating national minorities. I believe this assumption goes to the core of the meaning of Canadian sovereignty, especially Aboriginal sovereignty.

I want to point out, though, that there are two normative dimensions to Kymlicka's theory of minority rights and that it is important to keep them separate. First, there is the cultural dimension. Aboriginal cultures are unfairly vulnerable to influence by the dominant culture; for this reason, they are afforded special rights in order to protect their integrity. Aboriginal peoples constitute a kind of collective, and because of this their special rights are premised on two facts: that cultural membership is a primary good *and* that Aboriginal cultures are vulnerable to the unfair influences of the dominant culture. This is the broad context from which liberals have discussed the legitimacy of collective rights for groups.

The second normative dimension to Kymlicka's theory of minority rights involves the language of political sovereignty. Kymlicka does not use the word 'sovereignty'; even so, he brings the language of political sovereignty into his theory when he introduces the concept of national minorities. National minorities are defined as communities that were self-governing at the time of incorporation. Aboriginal communities constitute national minorities because normative weight is given to the fact that Aboriginal peoples occupied Canada first and therefore were self-governing societies. Thus the status of Aboriginal peoples as a national minority is based on the assumption that in the past they were self-governing, or sovereign.

Both these normative dimensions – cultural minority and national minority – are at work in Kymlicka's justification for Aboriginal rights of governance. However, liberals have discussed Aboriginal rights mostly in the language of cultural protection, rather than in the language of Aboriginal sovereignty. Kymlicka is right to raise the fact that Aboriginal peoples constitute a national minority, but there is no good reason for Aboriginal sovereignty – which is implicit in their status as a national minority – to disappear from the discussion of Aboriginal rights of governance in a contemporary context. If we take seriously the claim that Aboriginal peoples were self-governing nations before contact, we must reexamine our understandings of Aboriginal incorporation. This is because Aboriginal incorporation calls into question the nature of the formation of the Canadian state. Kymlicka is sensitive to the fact that Aboriginal peoples have suffered greatly throughout the history of the relationship; nonetheless, he sidesteps the issue of Aboriginal incorporation. Interestingly, the cultural and sovereignty dimensions of Kymlicka's theory both yield interpretations that advocate Aboriginal rights of governance, though I will claim that the second interpretation offers a more fruitful approach to capturing Aboriginal understandings of their sovereignty.

The cultural dimension of Kymlicka's theory does support Aboriginal sovereignty. Aboriginal peoples constitute a national minority; it follows that if our theory of justice deems it necessary, rights of governance can be accorded to them. Since culture is a primary good for all individuals, including Aboriginal individuals, the state ought to ensure policies that protect the integrity of all cultures. Since Aboriginal cultures are unfairly vulnerable to decimation by the overpowering dominant culture in Canada, justice demands that they be accorded special rights. Within a distributive theory of justice, these special rights *may* be rights of governance.

But it is important to note that the rights accorded to Aboriginal groups are justified only 'if there actually is a disadvantage with respect to cultural membership, and if the rights actually serve to rectify the disadvantage.' Kymlicka adds:

> One could imagine a point where the amount of land reserved for indigenous peoples would not be necessary to provide reasonable external protections, but rather would simply provide unequal opportunities to them. Justice would then require that the holdings of indigenous peoples be subject to the same redistributive taxation as the wealth of other advantaged groups, so as to assist the less well off in society. In the real

world, of course, most indigenous peoples are struggling to maintain the bare minimum of land needed to sustain the viability of their communities. But it is possible that their land holdings could exceed what justice allows.[24]

The point behind this passage, as Kymlicka explains in the accompanying footnote, is that he places Aboriginal rights squarely in a theory of distributive justice. Aboriginal cultures, as national minorities, can exercise their rights of governance only to the extent that they do not offset the balance of fairness in relation to the remaining cultures in Canada. This proviso leads to a weaker form of Aboriginal sovereignty because the rights of Aboriginal governance are recognized only to the extent that they do not trump the sovereignty of the Canadian state. Aboriginal peoples argue that limiting their rights in this ahistorical way misrecognizes the source of their right of governance.[25]

Aboriginal Incorporation and Aboriginal Sovereignty

Aboriginal perspectives must be included in the discourse that determines the meaning and content of their rights. We can retain the idea that Aboriginal communities are national minorities; but then we ought to focus on the problem of Aboriginal incorporation in order to determine the *current* political status of *particular* Aboriginal communities. This is because many Aboriginal communities maintain that they are *still* self-governing nations and that they have not in fact relinquished or ceded all of their powers to the state.[26] Aboriginal incorporation calls into question our understandings of Aboriginal peoples' political relationships with the Canadian state. From this perspective, Aboriginal rights of governance can be recognized in a much deeper sense than in the first interpretation. This is because Aboriginal sovereignty does not have to dissipate after the formation of the Canadian state; more importantly, it lies in the forefront of any current discussion about Aboriginal rights.

This indigenous approach differs from the first in that it facilitates a stronger conception of Aboriginal sovereignty, something like the one provided by the Gitxsan people, who believe that 'the ownership of territory is a marriage of the Chief and the land. Each Chief has an ancestor who encountered and acknowledged the life of the land. From such encounters come power. The land, the plants, the animals and the people all have spirit – they all must be shown respect. That is the basis of our law.'[27] The 'voice' that arises within a strong conception of Aboriginal sovereignty arises directly from the community itself – that is, from the people who hold the traditional knowledge of their community and who are recognized by their citizens as legitimately expressing the meaning of their political sovereignty.[28] However, for Canadian governments, recognition of a strong conception of Aboriginal sovereignty entails acceptance of the possibility that there are Aboriginal communities in Canada that remain sovereign political entities. Canadian governments have refused to recognize Aboriginal sovereignty in any form; until Aboriginal peoples participate as equals in the discourse that determines the meaning of their political sovereignty – and the rights of governance that follow from that sovereignty – legislative instruments and the meanings of rights as found in section 35(1) of the *Canadian Constitution* will remain undefined and elusive for policy makers.[29]

Of course, this does not bring us any closer to the meaning of Aboriginal sovereignty. The first step we must take to better understand what Aboriginal peoples themselves mean by sovereignty is to listen to their understandings of the historical relationship itself.[30] But it matters very much *how* we have this dialogue. For example, Kymlicka uses the word 'incorporation' to capture the historical significance of the early period of the relationship. This commits us to a particular interpretation of history. Such interpretations play pivotal roles in determining the meaning of Aboriginal sovereignty. The frustrating problem for Aboriginal peoples is that their interpretations of history have not been recognized as legitimate. I will return to this problem in chapter 5, but for now I want to focus on contemporary liberalism. A liberal theory of rights, in the context of Aboriginal peoples, functions ahistorically: it begins from a rationally constructed theory of distributive justice that bestows a set of fundamental rights on all individuals and, as a consequence, a set of special rights on individuals who belong to minority cultures. As I have tried to show by examining Kymlicka's theory of minority rights, it is possible for a version of liberalism to recognize that some Aboriginal communities are self-governing nations; what remains unresolved is a rich understanding of the meaning of Aboriginal sovereignty. This difference may not mean much to liberals and to Aboriginal policy makers, as a liberal theory of justice has in some sense distributed fairly special rights to Aboriginal peoples. However, sovereignty lies at the very core of Aboriginal existence, and history is the main source for understanding the complex nature of Aboriginal forms of political sovereignty.[31]

Kymlicka does allow historical interpretations to find their way into a liberal theory of justice when he invokes his second argument in favour of group-differentiated rights. The argument from historical agreement is meant to provide further normative support to the more fundamental equality argument, while addressing the issues surrounding the dissolution of Aboriginal sovereignty. Kymlicka points out that proponents of group-differentiated rights have had difficulty convincing opponents with historical arguments: 'Those people who think that group-differentiated rights are unfair have not been appeased by pointing to agreements that were made by previous generations in different circumstances, often undemocratically and in conditions of substantial inequality in bargaining power.' He goes on to ask: 'Why should not governments do what principles of equality require now, rather than what outdated and often unprincipled agreements require?'[32]

His answer is to question a fundamental assumption underlying the equality argument: 'The equality argument assumes that the state must treat its citizens with equal respect. But there is a prior question of determining which citizens should be governed by which states.'[33] For Aboriginal people like Harold Cardinal, this raises an extremely serious problem for liberalism. If we invoke the equality argument without looking at history, we gloss over the fact that Aboriginal peoples became citizens in many different ways, most of them unjust. More importantly, Aboriginal peoples in some communities simply are not citizens of the Canadian state.[34] Canadian political leaders, policy makers, and especially judges have unilaterally assumed that for better or worse, Canada's Aboriginal peoples have become citizens of Canada in the fullest sense. Essentially, this is how Kymlicka uses the term incorporation; his theory implicitly subsumes the fact that Aboriginal peoples have become citizens of the Canadian state and, more importantly, that they *may* have relinquished their original sovereignty in this process of incorporation.[35]

This is where Kymlicka's concept of incorporation becomes most useful for my investigation of Aboriginal sovereignty. If the incorporation process was unjust – as Kymlicka suggests was the case for many Aboriginal communities – we have to reassess the validity of Aboriginal incorporation in a much fuller investigation. It is not enough to leave the investigation with the claim that the incorporation was unjust and that therefore the Canadian state should accord Aboriginal peoples special rights to rectify past wrongs. This leads to Jeremy Waldron's view of 'superseding' historical injustice, which, along with Melvin

Smith's view of 'one law for all people,' treats Aboriginal peoples with a fundamental disrespect in that it does not allow them to speak for themselves.[36]

The relevant issue for Aboriginal peoples is not whether we ought to rectify past injustices in order to balance the scales of a liberal distributive justice system, but rather how governments can come to recognize the legitimacy of Aboriginal forms of sovereignty in order to renew the political relationship on more just foundations.[37] Kymlicka's theory can be interpreted in a way that at least makes room for Aboriginal peoples to speak for themselves. This is an important first step for liberalism, but it is only a first step. As I will try to show in the next two chapters, history and Western philosophy have not been kind to Aboriginal ways of understanding the world, so it is vital that Aboriginal voices be listened to and respected as philosophically legitimate participants in the discourse on Aboriginal sovereignty.

How this ought to happen is a serious practical and philosophical problem. European philosophers developed a discourse *about* Aboriginal peoples, and therefore their philosophical 'theories' did not require Aboriginal participation. This lack of philosophical participation is significant because it demonstrates that some Europeans in early colonial America cared little about Aboriginal ways of thinking.[38] I hope that by engaging in this investigation we may start on a path that examines the concept of Aboriginal sovereignty in a richer and more inclusive discourse.

To put it simply, if we want to understand better the meaning of what is commonly termed 'indigenous,' 'tribal,' or 'Aboriginal' sovereignty, we must *listen* to what Aboriginal peoples have to say about its meaning. This inclusion process, which itself requires explanation, does not mean that anything will actually get done in practice, or that enlightenment will automatically follow merely by including Aboriginal voices in legal and philosophical discourses. Aboriginal sovereignty is a normative political concept for several overlapping reasons: Aboriginal peoples assert it, constitutions recognize it, comprehensive and specific land claims are negotiated because of it, and public policies have been designed and implemented to undermine it. Yet Aboriginal peoples and the various Canadian governments cannot agree on the meaning of the political relationship itself. Defining or characterizing the relationship would go far towards situating Aboriginal understandings of political sovereignty.

I have attempted to argue in this chapter that Kymlicka's liberalism does not require the participation of Aboriginal peoples in order to determine the content of their 'special' rights. This is because Aboriginal rights are justified within a theory of distributive justice that does not fully recognize the legitimacy of Aboriginal sovereignty. Many Aboriginal people contend that their rights of governance flow from their political sovereignty and that these rights ought to be recognized by the Canadian governments (perhaps this is the significance of section 35(1). It is precisely this fact of Aboriginal experience that Canadian governments have refused to recognize in any serious fashion. I am suggesting that Kymlicka's theory of minority rights can be reformulated in a way that allows Aboriginal voices into the dominant, non-Aboriginal discourse on Aboriginal rights. However, to do so in a just way requires a re-examination of Aboriginal incorporation between Aboriginal peoples and the Canadian state. The meaning of Aboriginal incorporation is problematic because Aboriginal interpretations have not been recognized by the dominant colonial governments; therefore, it matters how we go about understanding its meaning. Like Cairns's view, the minority rights view does not require the participation of Aboriginal voices when the meaning and content of their rights are being deliberated. The problem of Aboriginal participation remains unresolved.

In the next two chapters, I examine what it means for Aboriginal peoples to participate more effectively in Canadian legal and political practices, especially those practices that determine the meaning of Aboriginal rights in Canada. The idea of Aboriginal participation, though, is a complex problem precisely because the relationship remains embedded in a colonial relationship. The Royal Commission on Aboriginal Peoples attempted to recognize the legitimacy of the nation-to-nation relationship. Whether RCAP's final report can resolve the problem of Aboriginal participation is quite another matter.

4 Word Warriors

The geese migrate because they have responsibilities to fulfil at different times and in different places. Before they fly they gather together and store up energy. I believe strongly that our people are gathering now, just like the geese getting ready to fly. I am tremendously optimistic that we will soon take on the responsibility we were meant to carry in the world at large.

Jim Bourque[1]

We are more than a curious medicine bundle on a museum rack ... We are tricksters in the blood, natural mixedblood tricksters, word warriors in that silence between bodies, and we bear our best medicine on our voices, in our stories.

Gerald Vizenor

As Canadians begin this millennium, understanding the meaning of Aboriginal rights, in both so-called theory and practice, will be one of our most immediate serious moral and political challenges. In this chapter, I discuss the role of Aboriginal peoples in asserting and protecting their rights, sovereignty, and nationhood within a Canadian constitutional democracy.[2] The contemporary legal and political relationship between Aboriginal peoples and the Canadian state is characterized as 'fiduciary" or 'trust-like' in nature.[3] In this chapter, I contend that if Aboriginal peoples' demands for recognition as self-determining political entities are to be realized, the legal and political practices that define and enforce the trust relationship will have to include Aboriginal practitioners in more substantive ways.

This chapter has two purposes. First, I explain what I mean for

Aboriginal peoples to 'participate' in Canadian legal and political practices. Second, I argue that before we can determine the meaning and content of a useful theory of Aboriginal rights in Canada, Aboriginal peoples will need to determine *who* ought to participate in those practices.[4] Who participates in mainstream academic and intellectual culture is problematic for indigenous peoples because indigenous forms of knowledge need to be reconciled with the legal and political discourses of the state; this necessitates a kind of division of intellectual labour in indigenous communities. A reconciliation must occur between 'indigenous philosophers' – indigenous intellectuals who possess the privileged forms of indigenous knowledge – and what I call 'word warriors,' whose primary function is to engage the legal and political discourses of the state.[5] In chapter 5, I will examine this relationship more closely and explore what it will entail for indigenous peoples to make greater inroads into mainstream Canadian legal and political practices while generating a more vigorous intellectual community.[6]

My discussion will fall into three sections. In the first, I briefly examine the final report of the Royal Commission on Aboriginal Peoples (RCAP) and show that the commission's work – an extensive, expensive quasi–listening exercise – was doomed to failure in at least in one regard.[7] For many Aboriginal peoples, the commission did not reconcile indigenous ways of knowing the world – expressed during the public hearings and much of the commission's research program – with contemporary Aboriginal legal and political practices in Canada. This is because indigenous forms of knowledge and the discourse of contemporary Aboriginal rights are at odds with respect to how they situate Aboriginal peoples in Canadian society. I am not suggesting that the commission did not try to reconcile these two seemingly disparate voices; I am saying they *could not* do so because of the very nature of the commission as a Canadian political institution.

I examine the final report's 'vision chapter' and show that the guiding principles of a renewed relationship (mutual recognition, mutual respect, sharing, and mutual responsibility) can be nothing more than a wish list without concomitant changes in public attitudes towards Aboriginal peoples and without some change in the ways their philosophies are included in contemporary Aboriginal legal and political practices. The commission was acutely aware of Aboriginal peoples' loss of voice in the political relationship, but the final report was unable to convince Parliament – and a large part of the Canadian public – that radical shifts in attitudes towards Aboriginal peoples were required before the relationship could be renewed on more just foundations.

In the second section, I explore a way of renewing the political relationship – a relationship that *must* include Aboriginal participation. If Aboriginal peoples are going to continue to assert that they possess unique forms of rights, sovereignty, and nationhood that the state must recognize as legitimate they will have to convince the dominant culture of the legitimacy of those assertions. This imperative raises the problem of how the forms of knowledge embedded in Aboriginal communities will ultimately be put to use in contemporary legal and political practices. More importantly, from an Aboriginal perspective, it raises the issue of who ought to participate in the state's contemporary legal and political discourses. This issue precludes the conversation about determining the meaning and content of Aboriginal rights because the kinds of explanations that are embedded in Aboriginal philosophies are not viewed as legitimate 'claims of reason' in contemporary legal and political discourses.

My argument is not a metaphysical one; that is, I am not claiming that Aboriginal ways of knowing the world are incommensurable with the legal and political discourses of the state. I *am* claiming that Aboriginal peoples must be more cautious about what they do with their ways of knowing the world, and especially with how they develop legal and political strategies for asserting, defending, and protecting the rights, sovereignty, and nationhood they still believe they possess. European-educated Aboriginal intellectuals have an uneasy relationship with indigenous forms of knowledge because they have been assigned the task of representing their communities (and often other indigenous communities) in the intellectual world of the dominant culture. The uneasiness this generates can be alleviated, although never entirely dissolved, provided they maintain strong connections to their communities. As long as Kymlicka's constraint requires indigenous peoples to explain themselves within the discourses of the dominant culture, there will be a need for specially educated indigenous people to generate the required explanations. It must be remembered that the need to explain ourselves to the dominant culture arises primarily for political reasons and only secondarily from a desire to attain some kind of rich cross-cultural understanding of indigenous philosophies.

The political philosophy of James Tully is useful for showing how political theorists and other concerned citizens can understand, not only the nature of the political relationship, but also how our participation in a particular kind of dialogue can enrich our self-understandings of who we are as participants in a just and coexistent relationship. I will discuss two complementary dimensions to Tully's political philosophy. One is his idea of 'a mediator' as a person who, in a political dialogue, is empowered to engage other participants in a respectful way. In *Strange Multiplicity*, Tully outlines a sophisticated way of looking at the evolution of European constitutional theory; in the process of his critical investigation he shows how it is possible for the Western tradition to accommodate Aboriginal voices on their own terms.[8]

The second dimension of Tully's work is his idea that political philosophy is a critical activity – that political thinking is a dialogical process between often competing participants, each vying to have its voice legitimated in the ongoing dialogue. This way of characterizing political philosophy embraces a practical, critical, and historical approach that incorporates aspects of Wittgenstein, the Cambridge School, Foucault, and other critical thinkers who think of political philosophy as an open-ended dialogue that involves a diversity of voices.[9] I defend this way of 'doing' political philosophy because it allows indigenous voices to participate in legal and political discourses *on their own terms*.

But Tully's philosophical approach is necessarily limited. He does not tell indigenous peoples *how* to participate in the ongoing dialogue of Aboriginal rights, sovereignty, and nationhood. From an Aboriginal perspective, as I noted earlier, in terms of indigenous participation, it matters who participates in ongoing dialogues. In the third section of this chapter, I contend that a community of indigenous intellectuals – word warriors – ought to assert and defend the integrity of indigenous rights and nationhood *and* protect indigenous ways of knowing within the existing legal and political practices of the dominant culture. However, their intellectual labour must be guided by indigenous philosophies; that is, indigenous philosophies – the wisdom of the elders – must inform and help shape the strategies word warriors use to engage European intellectual discourses. How they are to do so remains largely unresolved at this point in the relationship. What I am calling for is a kind of indigenous dialogue that protects the integrity of indigenous ways of knowing the world even while engaging the dominant intellectual culture in more empowering ways.

The primary political task of a community of word warriors, then, is to engage the legal and political discourses of the state in more serious ways.[10] Why? To me, the answer is simple: it is because our survival as sui generis political nations depends on it.[11] Aboriginal law and politics in Canada is quickly evolving into a highly sophisticated overlapping set of discourses.[12] Gaining expertise in Aboriginal legal and political issues necessarily involves learning complex legal, political, historical, and philosophical discourses. Word warriors must critically engage these discourses but must do so in accordance with indigenous ways of knowing the world. The difficult problem is to make better sense out of what we mean by 'acting in accordance' with indigenous ways of knowing. Furthermore, by making their way into the agonic intellectual community of the dominant culture – a community driven by non-Aboriginal institutions, interests, and methodologies – word warriors will be able to create stronger and more vibrant Aboriginal intellectual communities. Hopefully, in time, these people will help forge the necessary legal and political spaces that will allow indigenous forms of government – and consequently indigenous ways of being – to thrive within a more inclusive Canadian democratic state.

RCAP, Delgamuukw, and the Problem of Aboriginal Participation

I begin by citing 'Kymlicka's constraint': 'For better or worse, it is predominantly non-aboriginal judges and politicians who have the ultimate power to protect and enforce aboriginal rights, and so it is important to find a justification of them that such people can recognise and understand.'[13]

Aboriginal peoples have come to understand, only too well over the past few hundred years, the meaning of this imperative. The Royal Commission on Aboriginal Peoples (RCAP), an instrument of the federal government, was created (among other reasons) to seriously consider the meaning and content of Aboriginal rights in Canada. As I mentioned in the previous chapter, one important source of conflict was the issue of Aboriginal 'incorporation.' For many, Aboriginal incorporation is synonymous with the extinguishment of rights and nationhood; yet for Aboriginal peoples themselves, incorporation implies that they entered into treaty relationships on the premise that they would never surrender ownership of their lands.[14]

The issue of Aboriginal incorporation was the central legal and political dilemma the commission had to consider and was one of the main reasons the commission delayed its final report for over a year.[15] However, part of the reason for the impasse was related to how the commission was organized. Its mandate evolved through two broad phases.[16]

The first involved a massive listening and gathering exercise consisting of four rounds of public hearings. In addition, the commission had to draft and implement a comprehensive research plan. During the second phase, the commission was supposed to consolidate the material (evidence) gathered during the first phase and produce a comprehensive final report to be tabled in Parliament.[17]

The public hearings generated an overwhelming amount of information.[18] In this sense, it can be said that the commission listened to Aboriginal peoples. The commissioners, especially the non-Aboriginal ones, were profoundly affected by the testimony at the public hearings. The research program was also ambitious, extensive, and cutting edge. So there is no doubt that the commissioners had more than enough information to produce a useful final report. The problems for the commissioners began during the second phase, when they attempted to consolidate the material from the hearings and research with the existing legal and political practices of Aboriginal public policy in Canada.

The Aboriginal commissioners knew too well what life was like in Aboriginal communities, but they were not by any stretch of the imagination legal and political experts on the same level as the non-Aboriginal commissioners.[19] During phase II, the commission's focus shifted from engaging Aboriginal voices to engaging the language of public policy. As the commission's mandate unfolded, Aboriginal voices seemed to disappear, at least from the perspective of the Aboriginal commissioners and commission employees. Yet the commissioners persisted, and produced a report that arguably called for a vision of Canada that would return Aboriginal peoples to their rightful place in the Canadian social and political landscape.[20]

The last chapter of volume I of the final report, 'The Principles of a Renewed Relationship,' follows a historical re-evaluation of the relationship. In it, the commission argues that a new relationship cannot be renegotiated without a renewal of our understanding of the historical relationship. This chapter, originally called 'the vision chapter,' defends four principles that ought to guide the renewed relationship: mutual recognition, mutual respect, sharing, and mutual responsibility. The need for a renewed historical understanding has great philosophical and practical significance for a renewed political relationship because most Canadians need to change their attitudes towards Aboriginal peoples before just and effective policy changes can be initiated.

Mutual recognition 'calls on non-Aboriginal Canadians to recognize that Aboriginal people are the original inhabitants and caretakers of

events to occur. First, *as a matter of justice,* Canadian governments ought to recognize the nationhood of Aboriginal peoples and return portions of their lands to them. Second, *as a matter of justice,* Canadian governments ought to begin the process of empowering Aboriginal communities so that they can become more economically and politically self-sufficient. In the current relationship, Aboriginal peoples encounter uncompromising bureaucratic resistance to virtually every resource their communities require for their physical survival. The lesson that we have learned, and that history has shown Aboriginal peoples time and time again, is that even in the best of moral worlds, justice may demand a certain course of action but by no means guarantees it.[28]

According to the commission, the principles outlined in the vision chapter are what guided their recommendations on Aboriginal governance. That chapter reconciles the historical injustices articulated throughout volume I with the nation-to-nation political relationship and its governmental structures outlined in volume II. The vision chapter contains an imperative for all Canadians: if we want peaceful coexistence, attitudes towards Aboriginal peoples and their cultures must change. How to bring this change about in the public space, and especially within Canada's legal and political practices, is a serious issue with both philosophical and practical dimensions. The resolution must include a renewed respect for the integrity of Aboriginal peoples as legitimate political entities. The final report is a serious attempt to address this need, but its vision has not comprehensively woven the wisdom of the elders into its critiques of contemporary Aboriginal policy making in Canada. Many Canadians see the commission's recommendations as unreasonable and untenable in practice; many Aboriginal peoples think the commission's vision does not go far enough.

One reason why this vision has fallen short is that Royal Commissions, by definition, engage existing practices of governance and try to 'step back' from these practices in order to make policy recommendations to Parliament.[29] The commission was given a comprehensive mandate to examine virtually every part of Aboriginal life in Canada – the commissioners even had the power to subpoena witnesses. But in practice, the commission faced limits regarding what it could recommend. For example, it recommended that 'all governments in Canada recognize that Aboriginal peoples are nations vested with the right of self-determination.'[30] But this recommendation was weakened because the right of self-determination was embedded within the constitutional legitimacy of section 35(1). The idea that Aboriginal nations could legitimately secede from the Canadian state was not seriously considered by the commission:

> The right of self-determination is held by all the Aboriginal peoples of Canada, including First Nations, Inuit, and Metis people. It gives Aboriginal peoples the right to opt for a large variety of governmental arrangements *within* Canada, including some that involve a high degree of sovereignty. However, it does not entitle Aboriginal peoples to secede or form independent states, except in the case of grave oppression or a total disintegration of the Canadian state.[31]

The 'within Canada' imperative should not have been a problem for most Aboriginal nations, except that it placed legal and political limits on where the commission allocated its intellectual resources and ultimately on its recommendations for renewing the political relationship. In other words, the commission's legal and political imagination were firmly embedded in the idea that the sovereignty of the Canadian state was not to be questioned. The nation-to-nation political relationship was to be the cornerstone of a just and renewed relationship, but from the very beginning of the commission, the meaning and content of that relationship were limited in ways that ultimately set aside Aboriginal understandings of nationhood.

There are a number of ways that Aboriginal groups understand themselves as political nations. The concept of a 'nation' is a language game whose meaning in practice requires a complex investigation – one which respects that there are many possible definitions. The meaning of indigenous nationhood varies – for example, the Sechelt community views itself as a quasi-municipality in relation to the province of British Columbia, whereas the Iroquois Confederacy considers itself an international nation.[32] This diversity can only be unpacked by engaging in a dialogue with the indigenous nations themselves. One can hope that indigenous understandings of nationhood arrived at through dialogue with the state will give rise to forms of governance that respect indigenous participation. Of course, Aboriginal peoples remain hopeful. This doesn't guarantee that they will see positive results, but by engaging in a political dialogue, they will at least be able to speak for themselves.

The commission defended an *organic* model of governance, with Aboriginal peoples constituting one of three orders of government in Canada, alongside the provincial and federal governments. Even though it recognized Aboriginal peoples as nations, the commission privileged a model of Aboriginal governance that invoked a core/periphery hierarchy of governmental powers. This meant that the commission had to determine which inherent powers Aboriginal governments possessed and which powers could be limited by the legal and political relationship with the provincial and federal governments. The practical and philosophical problems associated with the core/periphery model were discussed only in the context of the Canadian state.[33] The commission's final report criticized Canadian legal and political institutions, but its primary function was to suggest new possibilities for governing Canada *as a nation-state*. Its main concern was with examining existing policies and making the political relationship better (especially given the Canadian governments' immoral behaviour during the Oka crisis of 1990). I am not suggesting that the commission's recommendations would not empower Aboriginal nations; I *am* saying that for cultural reasons, its mandate, while extensive, was limited as to what it could realistically analyse and recommend regarding the political relationship between the Canadian state and Aboriginal peoples.[34]

The commission's listening exercise was perhaps more successful because Aboriginal peoples could speak *on their own terms*. Most elders, and others who had something to say to the commissioners, believed in the commission's sincerity and good faith. But their language, and their 'claims of reason,' needed to be considered *on their own terms*. The commissioners were overwhelmed by the sheer volume and importance of the testimony given by Aboriginal peoples. Also, they were unable to reconcile Aboriginal claims of reason with what they believed – or at least what they initially believed – were their tasks at hand as commissioners. Their *political* task was to generate sound policy recommendations to Parliament – recommendations that would renew on more just foundations the legal and political place of Aboriginal peoples in Canadian society. Their *moral* task was to reconcile Canada's colonial past with a richer renewed vision of Canadian society – a vision that would return a voice to Aboriginal peoples and give that voice prominence. The commission never succeeded in reconciling the political and moral dimensions of its mandate. Canada's great vision remains unfinished and unarticulated.

The tension between the need for sound policy recommendations and the need for a renewed moral commitment to Aboriginal peoples buttressed two broadly defined public attitudes towards Aboriginal peoples. First, there were those who saw RCAP's final report as simply wrong, misguided, unrealistic, or in the least far too progressive. White Paper liberals believe that Aboriginal peoples and their rights are unquestionably subsumed in the Canadian political landscape and that it is nonsense to think that Aboriginal peoples might be 'nations.' Just as the White Paper initiated a shift in Aboriginal rights discourse in Canada, RCAP's final report propelled (once again) White Paper liberalism to the forefront of Canadian politics.

Then there were those who believed that RCAP did not go far enough in defining the content of Aboriginal rights, sovereignty, and nationhood in Canada. As I mentioned earlier, the nation-to-nation political relationship remains undefined, especially in the context of section 35(1). Most Canadians endorse one of two broad views: either Aboriginal peoples possess special rights, or they don't. But the significance of this dichotomy for existing legal and political practices – especially in terms of the landscape of rights created out of the historical and political dialogues between these opposing views – has evolved in ways that continue to marginalize Aboriginal peoples.[35]

Yet Aboriginal peoples continue to defend their unique status in the legal and political relationship.[36] The main source of Aboriginal rights discourse in Canada is section 35(1) of the *Canadian Constitution*, although the discourse is also shaped by existing treaty relationships, several comprehensive land agreements, the *Indian Act*, and the many ongoing political negotiations that various Aboriginal peoples are conducting with the federal and provincial governments. It is no secret that for Aboriginal peoples to participate effectively in Canadian legal and political cultures, they must engage the normative discourses of the state. This means that their defences for their views, and their justifications for a place at the table, are articulated using the discourses of rights, sovereignty, and nationhood. Aboriginal peoples have become adept at using these discourses to defend their positions; even so, there remains a fundamental asymmetry in the legal and political relationship.[37]

Indigenous peoples have their own philosophies, which they apply when articulating their understandings of the world. Indigenous philosophies are rooted in oral traditions, which generate explanations of the world expressed in indigenous normative languages. But the legal and political discourses of the state do not use indigenous philosophies to justify their legitimacy. The asymmetry arises because indigenous peoples must use the normative language of the dominant culture to ultimately defend world views that are embedded in completely different normative frameworks. The dominant culture does not face this hurdle. This is essentially another way of invoking Kymlicka's constraint. Part of listening to Aboriginal peoples, and thereby facilitating greater Aboriginal participation, must involve overcoming this asymmetry.

The Supreme Court, in its now famous *Delgamuukw* decision, purportedly offered some hope. Although the Court ordered a retrial for technical reasons, one of its central findings was that Canadian courts must find ways to accommodate Aboriginal oral histories as authentic sources of historical evidence.[38] The case was supposed to decide 'the nature and scope of the constitutional protection afforded by s. 35(1) to common law aboriginal title.'[39] However, when the meaning and content of Aboriginal title in common law were being determined, the problem of incorporating Aboriginal understandings of political sovereignty became subsumed in the Court's claim that 'Aboriginal title is a burden on the Crown's underlying title before that title existed. The Crown, however, did not gain this title until it asserted sovereignty and it makes no sense to speak of a burden on the underlying title before that title existed. Aboriginal title crystallized at the time sovereignty was asserted.'[40]

From an Aboriginal perspective, this raises the issue of the legitimacy of the initial formation of the Canadian state. This problem does not arise for the Court since the legitimacy of Canadian sovereignty is not up for negotiation; the real issues for the Court centre on how best to accommodate the concept of aboriginal title in existing Canadian law.

Many believe that the Court has potentially created the legal space for Aboriginal oral histories to play a role in supporting Aboriginal legal arguments, thus providing a respectful bridge between indigenous ways of understanding the world and normative Aboriginal rights discourse in Canada. But on closer examination, we see that Aboriginal oral histories can be used only in a very narrow way; the Court has decreed they can only be used to justify title – a form of land tenure that is recognized and bestowed by the state. In other words, they cannot be used in a way that Aboriginal people have been demanding, which is to recognize a form of ownership embedded in a richer understanding of indigenous nationhood.

Aboriginal title is a right to the land itself, but its place in the landscape of Aboriginal rights discourse has been shaped mostly by another important Supreme Court decision: *R v. Van der Peet*.[41] When *Delgamuukw* is contextualized by *Van der Peet* we see that Aboriginal title is constrained by Eurocentric understandings of culture, and especially by Eurocentric understandings of indigenous cultures. *Van der Peet* is important because the Court was supposed to provide guidance 'concerning the test it would use to identify those [Aboriginal rights] protected by section 35(1).'[42] The Court, while supposedly making room for Aboriginal forms of evidence in determining the content of an Aboriginal right, was dictating the language through which the evidence was to be articulated and understood.

The Court stated:

> To be an aboriginal right an activity must be an element of a practice, custom or tradition integral to a distinctive culture of the aboriginal group claiming the right. A number of factors must be considered in applying the 'integral to a distinctive culture' test. The court must take into account the perspective of the aboriginal peoples, *but that perspective must be framed in terms cognizable to the Canadian legal and constitutional structure.*[43]

One problem is that the 'integral to a distinctive culture' test links the content of Aboriginal rights to Eurocentric ideas of what indigenous cultures – and thus practices, and ultimately rights – ought to look like. Justice L'Heureux Dubé, in her dissenting opinion, wrote:

> Most importantly, aboriginal rights protected under s. 35(1) must be interpreted in the context of the history and culture of the specific aboriginal society and in a manner that gives the rights meaning to the natives. It is not appropriate that the perspective of the common law be given an equal weight with the perspective of the natives.[44]

The way the Court has set up the discussion about whether a practice counts as a constitutional right is now limited by the imperative that if indigenous philosophies, embedded in indigenous languages, are to play a normative role in determining the scope of rights protected in section 35(1), they must be articulated in the legal and political discourses of the state. The purpose of the *Delgamuukw* and *Van der Peet* decisions was not to begin a cross-cultural conversation about the meaning of sovereignty or political legitimacy; rather, the Court's primary concern was to develop a short list of Aboriginal rights as constitutional rights and to be very clear about how these rights can be limited in practice, and more importantly, how the state can legitimately infringe on those rights.

So, what exactly *is* the problem at hand? Aboriginal explanations of rights, sovereignty, and nationhood, which admittedly are rooted in oral traditions, need to be integrated more respectfully into the existing legal and political practices of the state. This problem is both philosophical and practical. It is philosophical in the sense that we need to understand better how radically different ways of understanding the world can have a respectful, useful conversation about the meaning and content of rights, sovereignty, and nationhood. It is practical because we do not know exactly what the relationship ought to look like between indigenous oral traditions and the legal and political discourses of the state. In the next section of this chapter I address the philosophical dimension of the problem; in the final section I will turn to the practical dimension.

Mediators

In his 1995 book *Strange Multiplicity*, James Tully examines the 'politics of cultural recognition' in the context of how constitutionalism has evolved in European political thought.[45] In his philosophical investigation, he engages an indigenous political vision in the form of Haida artist Bill Reid's sculpture *The Spirit of Haida Gwaii*. It is worth quoting Tully's description in full:

> The sculpture is a black bronze canoe, over nineteen feet in length, eleven feet wide, and twelve feet high, containing thirteen passengers, *sghaana* (spirits or myth creatures) from Haida mythology. *Xuuwaji*, the bear mother, who is part human, and bear father sit facing each other at the bow with their two cubs between them. *Ttsaang*, the beaver, is paddling menacingly amidships, *qqaaxhadajaat*, the mysterious, intercultural dogfish woman, paddles just behind him and *Qaganjaat*, the shy but beautiful mouse woman is tucked in the stern. *Ghuuts*, the ferociously playful wolf, sinks his fangs in the eagle's wing and *ghuut*, the eagle seems to be attacking the bear's paw in retaliation. *Hlkkyaan qqusttaan*, the frog, who symbolizes the ability to cross boundaries (*xhaaidla*) between worlds is, appropriately enough, partially in and out of the boat. Further down in the canoe, the ancient reluctant conscript, brought on board from Carl Sandburg's poem, 'Old Timers,' paddles stoically (up to a point). *Xuuya*, the legendary raven – the master of tricks, transformations and multiple identities – steers the canoe as her or his whim dictates. Finally in the centre of this motley crew, holding the speaker's staff in his right hand, stands the *Kitslaani*, the chief or exemplar, whose identity, due to his kinship to the raven (often called *Nangkilstlas*, the One who gives orders), is uncertain. *Bill Reid asks of the*

chief, 'Who is he? That's the big question.' So the chief has come to be called 'Who is he?' or 'Who is he going to be?[46]

Through the course of his book, Tully uncovers a complex intellectual landscape out of which contemporary debates in constitutional theory have evolved. He cites three conventions found in common constitutionalism: mutual recognition, continuity, and consent. In the context of the Aboriginal–European newcomer political relationship, mutual recognition means to recognize and accommodate the fact that Aboriginal peoples constitute equal and self-governing nations. This relationship was first manifested in the early treaties. The second convention, continuity, means that Aboriginal nations did not relinquish their sovereignty when they entered into treaty relationships with the Crown. The convention of continuity has been superseded by the unilaterally imposed practice of discontinuity or extinguishment. The third convention, consent, is intimately related to the two other conventions. Consent demands that any changes in the political relationship that affect the nature of the relationship require the consent of the concerned parties. This is embedded in one of the oldest conventions in democratic political thought – *quod omnes tangit ab omnibus comprobetur* – 'what touches all should be agreed to by all.'[47]

Tully argues, as did the commission in its 'vision chapter,' that these fundamental conventions, already embedded in constitutional practice, must guide contemporary constitutional practices if we are to embrace diversity in its richest form. Peaceful coexistence among conflicting voices is possible, but only from within a dialogical relationship:

> A mediated peace is a just peace: just because it is a constitutional settlement in accord with the three conventions of justice and peaceful because the constitution is accommodated to the diverse needs of those who agree to it. If this view of constitutionalism came to be accepted, the allegedly irreconcilable conflicts of the present would not have to be the tragic history of our future.[48]

According to Tully, a just constitutional relationship, guided by the three conventions, is negotiated, and renegotiated, between the participants.

Political relationships, like the one characterized in *The Spirit of Haida Gwaii*, are negotiated relationships in which 'the passengers vie and negotiate for recognition and power.' The leader – the chief – plays a specific role in this kind of political relationship. Tully's last two sentences of *Strange Multiplicity* are prophetic: 'Of equal importance to their pacific way of life, they also never fail to heed what is said by the chief whose identity has remained a mystery until this moment. She or he is the mediator.'[49] The mediator, for Tully, embraces the three conventions of constitutionalism – the four principles defended in the 'vision chapter' – and facilitates them in political practice. Another important quality of the mediator is that she or he is able to guide others regarding how to act appropriately in this complex politics of cultural recognition.

Tully's book is ultimately an appeal to leadership: it is offered primarily as a way for non-Aboriginal people to understand constitutional relationships with a diversity of politically recognized participants. A non-Aboriginal mediator recognizes and respects the legitimacy of Aboriginal ways of thinking and living and weaves them into her own philosophical attitudes. Mediators, then, engage the legal and political discourses of the state, guided by richer and more inclusive sets of assumptions about Aboriginal peoples, political sovereignty, and especially political recognition. One virtue of Tully's approach is that the meaning of Aboriginal incorporation becomes embedded in the discourse and practices of the negotiated relationship itself. Aboriginal explanations of incorporation are central to the evolving legal and political discourses of Aboriginal rights and sovereignty *because* the normative language of the dialogue and its consequences in practice are always contested between the negotiating parties.

The most important and also the most complex convention is that of mutual recognition. Aboriginal peoples' ways of thinking about and understanding the world are not recognized by most non-Aboriginal people as of equal value to European philosophical traditions.[50] As long as Kymlicka's constraint remains imposed on Aboriginal peoples, this will always be so. If Aboriginal peoples take this fact of the relationship seriously, and I certainly do, then Aboriginal intellectuals must reconsider how Aboriginal ways of thinking about the world ought to be brought to the negotiation table, to the Supreme Court, and into university classrooms.

Tully shows that Canadians should hold on to their most valued political conventions but must also renew them in the agonic political reality of late-twentieth-century Canadian politics. He uses an Aboriginal example to drive home the point that every just political relationship is always contested and therefore requires people to negotiate in accordance with the three time-tested conventions of the European constitutional tradition. Tully's vision, while deeply respectful of Aboriginal political thinking, is necessarily incomplete. This 'incompleteness,' though, is a virtue because it leaves philosophical dialogues as ongoing activities wherein meaning is constantly contested and renegotiated; and it is through the dialogical process that the participants can gain insight into the value of the critical activity itself. Tully argues that approaching political problems in this way allows marginalized voices to participate legitimately in shaping the normative language of philosophical discourses and that their claims of reason can play a significant role in transforming the governing practices that have been called into question.[51]

The question of how Aboriginal peoples can come to sit at the table with political philosophers *and* with political leaders goes to the core of Tully's political thought and also of Bill Reid's. With regard to the state fully recognizing the legitimacy of Aboriginal rights in Canada, the three conventions of modern constitutionalism have not been completely ignored over the past thirty years. This is in part because of the rise of six types of critical study that have made inroads into mainstream political thinking:

> Philosophers of multiculturalism, multinationalism, indigenous rights, and constitutional pluralism have thrown critical light on struggles over recognition and accommodation of cultural diversity within and across the formerly free and equal institutions of constitutional democracies ... Finally, postcolonial and postmodern scholars have drawn attention to the various ways our prevailing logocentric languages of political reflection fail to do justice to the multiplicity of different voices striving for the freedom to have an effective democratic say over the ways they are governed as a new century dawns.[52]

Indigenous peoples have had *some* influence in shaping the practices of governance that effect the interpretation and implementation of their rights, but we are far from being recognized as what the commission calls 'partners in confederation.'[53] Tully's mediators have more inclusive attitudes towards Aboriginal participation and view the political dialogues over meaning as contested ongoing conversations that respect the integrity of the participating voices. In the next section I examine more closely the idea of a community of word warriors, and especially the place they occupy in indigenous and Canadian societies.

Word Warriors

It is common knowledge in many indigenous communities that for a boy to become a man he must have a vision. That is, he must discover, or be shown, what his purpose is in life. This involves a long process of learning the physical and spiritual landscapes he has inherited from his ancestors. A vision quest reminds one of the importance of listening to our world. The survival of indigenous communities depends on individuals accepting their responsibilities, but they cannot do so unless they have learned the necessary survival skills. Surviving in the sometimes hostile world requires finely developed skills and knowledge, which need to function properly. Among the Anishnabi people, elders taught children the necessary skills for survival, along with the stories that made sense of their world, passed on as tribal knowledge. They taught hunting, trapping, and other practical skills alongside creation stories, moral and political philosophy, and cosmology. This was the Anishnabi way and it worked well for countless generations.[54]

At this time in our history, what kind of vision does an Anishnabi require? A vision seeks understanding of the diverse landscapes in which one is inextricably immersed. The brutal reality is that these landscapes have changed drastically since the arrival of Europeans. What has not changed for the Anishnabi is the need to survive in a sometimes hostile world. These landscapes are still shared with Anishnabi ancestors, but the tools for survival have had to change. No doubt, the responsibilities one must embrace to secure the survival of the community still require special skills and knowledge. Much of the indigenous knowledge required for survival, and many of the skills, have been passed on to the youth by special people in traditional ways, usually by older family members in the community. But colonialism has created other types of landscapes that our ancestors would have found incomprehensible.[55]

Unfortunately, there are intellectual landscapes that have been forced on Aboriginal peoples – for example, the languages of rights, sovereignty, and nationalism. These intellectual traditions, stained by colonialism, have created discourses on property, ethics, political sovereignty, and justice that have subjugated, distorted, and marginalized Aboriginal ways of thinking. Throughout the history of the relationship, these Eurocentric discourses have created for Aboriginal peoples an intellectual landscape that in some cases has been purposefully designed to exclude Aboriginal ways of thinking.[56]

The knowledge and skills required to participate in the legal and political discourse of Aboriginal rights in Canada are now, for better or worse, a significant part of Aboriginal life. Over the past thirty years, the discourse on Aboriginal rights has evolved without a significant contribution by Aboriginal intellectuals; the effects of this on Aboriginal communities have been devastating. Aboriginal peoples now view these Eurocentric legal and political discourses with scepticism and contempt and often consider embracing them to be a sign of assimilation. There is an element of good reason to this prevailing attitude, but if Aboriginal peoples want to survive as distinct political communities, they will need to use these intellectually imposed landscapes more effectively.

By using these intellectual landscapes in more meaningful and effective ways, we will be expressing what Osage English professor Robert Allen Warrior calls our 'intellectual sovereignty':

> If our struggle is anything, it is a way of life. That way of life is not a matter of defining a political ideology or having a detached discussion about the unifying structures and essences of American Indian traditions. It is a decision – a decision we make in our minds, in our hearts, and in our bodies – to be sovereign and to find out what that means in the process.[57]

Warrior contends that American Indian intellectual sovereignty is not dependent on the dominant culture; we have the power to speak for ourselves, we just need to decide to do it. Warrior argues that American Indian intellectuals have

> by and large [been] caught in a death dance of dependence between, on the one hand, abandoning ourselves to the intellectual strategies and categories of white, European thought and, on the other hand, declaring that we need nothing outside ourselves and our cultures in order to understand the world and our place in it.[58]

He optimistically adds:

> When we remove ourselves from this dichotomy, much becomes possible. We see first that the struggle for sovereignty is not a struggle to be free from the influence of anything outside ourselves, but a process of asserting the power we possess as communities and individuals to make decisions that affect our lives.[59]

This last comment is worthy of closer examination, especially in the context of the meaning of Aboriginal rights in Canada.

Warrior seems to be suggesting that in the end, expressing our intellectual sovereignty requires us to assert a power we already possess. In one sense he is right; that is, in the end it is up to us to assert our ways of knowing the world, and we have to decide as a community how to do so. But there is another aspect to this ultimately unilateral assertion of intellectual sovereignty, especially when we consider the contemporary legal and political discourse of Aboriginal rights. This is the fact that by and large, the non-Aboriginal legal and political intellectual community does not recognize indigenous intellectual traditions as valuable sources of knowledge (never mind wisdom). Our 'tribal secrets' are of anthropological or historical interest only – most non-Aboriginal academics are still more interested in generating a discourse *about* Aboriginal peoples than in defending, say, the epistemological value of indigenous ways of knowing. Aboriginal understandings of the world are given little if any attention in the contemporary legal and political culture.

Of course, this does not mean that indigenous ways of knowing are not valuable sources of knowledge. But it is not enough for indigenous intellectuals to assert their intellectual sovereignty in the already vigorous, agonic mainstream intellectual community. *As a matter of survival,* Aboriginal intellectuals must engage the non-Aboriginal intellectual landscapes from which their political rights and sovereignty are articulated and put to use in Aboriginal communities. I am suggesting that instead of carving out their own communities and asserting their intellectual sovereignty within them, Aboriginal intellectuals must develop a community of practitioners *within* the existing dominant legal and political intellectual communities, while remaining an essential part of a thriving indigenous intellectual community.

For example, since the *Calder* decision in 1972, Aboriginal legal theory in Canada has been moving in new directions. Douglas Sanders, Brian Slattery, Russel Barsh, Bruce Clark, Patrick Macklem, Kent McNeil, and others – all non-Aboriginal legal scholars – have over the past thirty years established 'Native law' as a sophisticated specialty within the broader field of law.[60] At the same time, Aboriginal legal scholars such as Mary Ellen Turpel, Sakej Henderson, Patricia Montour, Mark Dockstator, John Borrows, Darlene Johnston, and Gordon Christie have created a stronger Aboriginal presence in the same field. These Aboriginal intellectuals are engaging the discourse of Aboriginal rights in creative and sophisticated ways even while remaining connected to their communities. We can hope that as more and more Aboriginal people become experts in Aboriginal legal studies, they will gain public recognition as the intellectual authorities on Aboriginal law in Canada.[61]

Other disciplines need to follow suit. For example, Bruce Trigger makes a similar plea in the context of professional historians and anthropologists:

> While Native people have played the major political role in challenging the image that other Native Americans have of them, non-aboriginal historians and anthropologists have been working to dispel myths that their predecessors helped to create ... It is essential that more Native people who are interested in studying their past should become professional historians and anthropologists, so that their special insights and perspectives can contribute to the study of Native history ... so the distinction between professional anthropologists and historians on the one hand and Native people on the other should give way to disciplines in which Native people play an increasingly important role. Such collegiality will mark the beginning of a new phase in the study of Native history.[62]

Of course, these are long-term goals for Aboriginal peoples. A major problem with increasing the Aboriginal presence in the academic community is that, for most Aboriginal students, the university remains a hostile environment. Most of the course content encountered by Aboriginal students at universities focuses on Aboriginal peoples as objects of study. Many Aboriginal university students still experience residential-school attitudes, and therefore most do not finish their degrees. Trigger's collegial community would consist of well-educated, publishing PhD's; unfortunately, most Aboriginal students do not graduate from high school. Nonetheless, Trigger's point is well worth taking, and I believe it can be *one* important way of empowering Aboriginal peoples. If this is true, then the problem is *how* to establish a thriving Aboriginal intellectual community. This will be especially difficult in more conservative fields such as law, philosophy, economics, and political science.

That such an intellectual community is needed is a sad, brutal consequence of the Aboriginal–European newcomer relationship. For far too long, Aboriginal peoples have had to use European discourses of rights to explain their place in the political relationship. To renew the relationship by returning Aboriginal voices to their rightful place will take some time. Following Neurath, we will have to rebuild our ship while we are still at sea – one plank at a time. For word warriors to fulfil their responsibilities effectively, they will have to know their way around European intellectual traditions *and* know how these traditions have affected Aboriginal intellectual landscapes. Finally, their intellectual labour will have to be useful. That is, the intellectual community will have to be part of a larger and more effective indigenous political machinery, one that is able to assert and protect the rights we believe we possess.

Of course, this is an optimistic view of indigenous intellectual culture. Aboriginal leadership has always been diverse. Taiaiake Alfred writes, regarding the dilemma of contemporary Native leadership, that the issue is, 'Whether to seek internal peace by meeting the needs of the community and restoring it to strength and health, or to promote stability in relations with others by satisfying the demands and expectations of mainstream society.'[63] Word warriors focus on the second of these alternatives, while necessarily meeting the needs of the community. Historically, our leaders have had to be historians, lawyers, anthropologists, philosophers, and politicians in order to be listened to by the dominant society. A community of word warriors, representing many nations, can focus outwards and find ways of making inroads into the dominant intellectual, legal, and political communities in Canada. Nonetheless, the relationship between Aboriginal leaders and a community of word warriors is going to be fraught with difficulties, in terms of the philosophical complexity of the relationship, and also in terms of how word warriors will be situated *between* the indigenous and European worlds.[64]

This is where Tully's notion of a mediator is helpful. He is offering a way for philosophers, especially political philosophers, to see their own field of study in a way that includes – indeed, even demands – Aboriginal participation. But his mediator necessarily engages an Aboriginal mediator. An Aboriginal mediator – a word warrior – is an indigenous person who engages the imposed legal and political discourses of the state guided by the belief that the knowledge and skills to be gained by engaging in such discourses are necessary for the survival of all indigenous peoples.

Tully's mediator and the indigenous word warrior both inhabit a social space that is difficult to define. Indigenous intellectuals must be citizens of an indigenous community, but how they will manage to move between languages, between ways of thinking about the world, remains to be determined in practice. Clearly, though, word warriors will have to assert and protect those ways of knowing the world that define indigenous peoples. This may well be a difficult task in a some-times hostile world, but it is what we will need to do. Perhaps Edward Said's idea of an intellectual as an exile is useful here: 'the exilic intellec-tual does not respond to the logic of the conventional but to the audac-ity of daring, and to representing change, to moving on, not standing still.' Later on he adds: 'Nothing in my view is more reprehensible than those habits of mind in the intellectual that induce avoidance, that characteristic turning away from a difficult and principled position which you know to be the right one, but which you decide not to take.'[65]

I have written this chapter under the assumption that greater partici-pation in the intellectual culture of the dominant culture is a good thing, because having our voices heard is the first step towards having a greater say in shaping the normative language of contemporary Ab-original politics. Word warriors are the 'class' of indigenous people that will make these intellectual inroads into the dominant world, so it matters just who does this kind of intellectual labour. There are many questions one can ask about this kind of person, but I have not yet asked *how* word warriors will come to hold these intellectual positions of authority. The word warrior's most difficult task will be to reconcile indigenous ways of knowing with the forms of knowledge that define European intellectual traditions. This is not an anthropological exercise; rather, it represents a kind of vision quest of its own: the unfolding of the investigation itself will reveal how we ought to understand the world and how we see ourselves in the world. Like those of pipe carriers, the duties and responsibilities of word warriors will be exten-sive; like pipe carriers, word warriors will best be chosen carefully and raised from a very early age to fulfil their duties to their communities.

In the final chapter I take a closer look at what it means for Aboriginal peoples to 'tell our own stories in our own ways.' Who tells these stories matters, and how they are told matters – especially for Aboriginal peoples. An indigenous intellectual community is a peculiar commu-nity because indigenous intellectuals engage the intellectual world of the dominant culture while embracing the indigenous ways of knowing the world found in their communities. In the final chapter I ask this important question: 'How should indigenous peoples be thinking about the necessary division of intellectual labour that, I believe, is required in order for indigenous peoples to survive *as distinct peoples*?'

5 Towards a Critical Indigenous Philosophy

We have discarded our broken arrows and our empty quivers, for we know what served us in the past can never serve us again ... It is only with tongue and speech that I can fight my people's war.

Chief Dan George

Speaking the truth to power is no Panglossian idealism: it is carefully weighing the alternatives, picking the right one, and then intelligently representing it where it can do the most good and cause the right change.

Edward Said

I began this book with a discussion of the White Paper, which Aboriginal peoples hold up as a paradigm example of colonialism under the guise of renewing the political relationship on more just liberal foundations. Subsequent attempts by Alan Cairns and Will Kymlicka to re-shape liberalism while respecting the legitimacy of Aboriginal rights failed to address the central problem with White Paper liberalism: its failure to accommodate and respect Aboriginal voices on their own terms. More importantly, contemporary theories of Aboriginal rights continue to marginalize Aboriginal peoples' philosophical views of justice. The Royal Commission on Aboriginal Peoples was acutely aware of this problem, not only in theory, but also in Canadian legal and political practices. RCAP's 'vision' of the renewed treaty relationship returned Aboriginal peoples to their rightful place in the relationship but had little to say about *how* this renewal was to take hold in main-stream Canadian society. Canadians need to be convinced that the nation-to-nation relationship is *the* just form of political relationship with Aboriginal peoples; generating cogent and useful defences for this position is one of the most difficult challenges facing those who support Aboriginal rights in Canada.

I have not provided yet another 'theory' of how the relationship between Aboriginal peoples and the Canadian state ought to look and evolve, because the question of *who* ought participate in the legal and political practices that determine the meaning and content of Aboriginal rights in Canada precludes the proffering of moral and political theories of justice. It matters who participates because the form and content of the difference (for lack of a better word, of our 'indigeneity') that Aboriginal peoples are demanding Canadian governments recognize must be explained to non-Aboriginal people. At least at this point in history, Kymlicka's constraint is a reality that indigenous peoples have to address. I have suggested that 'word warriors' are in the best position to engage these non-indigenous legal and political practices simply because they have been educated in the dominant culture's intellectual community and therefore ought to be more familiar with its discourses. More to the point, word warriors ought to be intimately familiar with the legal and political discourses of the state, and therefore able to use them to assert, defend, and protect the rights, sovereignty, and nationhood of indigenous communities.

But this form of participation generates an uneasy tension within indigenous communities. This tension arises because we are not at all clear about how the division of intellectual labour ought to be understood within indigenous communities and consequently how our ways of understanding the world ought to be expressed to the dominant culture. An indigenous intellectual culture needs to address what it means to claim that indigenous peoples have unique ways of understanding the world, and that those differences matter both legally and politically. At the same time, that culture must insist on greater participation by indigenous people in what have been historically exclusively non-indigenous intellectual practices.

I contend that the *philosophical* relationship between indigenous ways of knowing the world and the legal and political discourses of the state has evolved within the ongoing political relationship.[1] That is, the very ways that we frame the language of rights, sovereignty, and nationalism are also steeped in colonialism; yet, like the political relationship, indigenous resistance has weathered these discourses. A critical indigenous philosophy must unpack the colonial framework of these discourses, assert and defend our 'indigeneity' within the dominant culture, and defend the legal and political integrity of indigenous communities.

The following discussion has three sections. First, I outline three kinds of indigenous intellectual projects. There are radical differences between those who 'do' indigenous philosophy, those indigenous peoples who engage European philosophy on its own terms, and word warriors who engage European philosophy for the purposes of defending indigenous rights, sovereignty, and nationhood. Second, I lay out in a general way what I consider the most important activities of a critical indigenous philosophy. Indigenous intellectuals must participate in three distinct activities: (a) they must take up, deconstruct, and continue to resist colonialism and its effects on indigenous peoples; (b) they must protect and defend indigeneity; and (c) they must engage the legal and political discourses of the state in an effective way. Third and finally, I discuss where I situate my own work and how European-educated indigenous philosophers can participate in a richer and more empowered indigenous intellectual community.

The intellectual battleground on which word warriors contend is located deep in the dominant culture. Its intellectual landscapes continue to have political significance for indigenous peoples. For example, the languages of rights, sovereignty, and nationalism have evolved over the past few centuries with very little indigenous participation. As both Cairns and Kymlicka have argued, any special political rights that indigenous peoples may possess can be subsumed within already existing Eurocentric political theories of justice. To engage in a critical dialogue over the meaning and content of Aboriginal rights in Canada, as they are understood in section 35(1) of the *Canadian Constitution*, is a political process that embraces a *philosophical* process.

First, what do we mean by European philosophy? Finding agreement among European and North American philosophers about the meaning of philosophy is a daunting if not impossible task. The point I make for now is that even though its boundaries are difficult to ascertain, a distinct European philosophical community exists, one in which indigenous representation is astonishingly low.[2] So it makes sense to claim that at this time in the relationship, any indigenous inroads into the philosophical community are going to be by individuals, not by an empowered intellectual community. Yet it is important that word warriors function as part of a politicized intellectual community. This turns the problem of how indigenous intellectuals can participate effectively in an academic field like philosophy, while retaining strong connections to their communities, into a practical (and politicized) one, not just a philosophical one.

Examining the relationship between African philosophy and Western European philosophy may provide some instructive insight for developing a North American indigenous intellectual context. For various reasons, African philosophy has had for more than a century a relationship with European philosophical discourse, especially with regard to analysis of European colonialism.[3] African philosophy is a kind of indigenous philosophy, and the problem of reconciling its traditional forms of knowledge with those of the modern world has been central to African intellectual culture. Kwame Anthony Appiah, in his important and influential book *In My Father's House: Africa in the Philosophy of Culture*, writes about the complex interweaving among 'African philosophy,' European philosophy (he is a Princeton philosophy professor), his own Asante culture, and Christianity – to name a few of the diverse forms that Appiah embraces.[4] In reflecting on the meaning of 'Black' or 'African' philosophy he asks:

> What account can we give, then, of the belief that there is a role for something that is importantly African to be done in philosophy? Part of the explanation must lie ... in racialism: what more natural reaction to a European culture that claims – with Hume and Hegel – that the intellect is the property of white skins, than to insist there is something important in the sphere that belongs to black men? If there is white philosophy, why not also black philosophy? The origins of the argument are intelligible – and that it is somehow healthier than the view of the apostles of negritude, that black men should give the intellect over to whites and explore the affective realm that is their special property.[5]

He immediately rejects the idea that black philosophy gains its legitimacy by comparing itself to European philosophy. European philosophy is important to the history of ideas but does not have privileged access to the truth. He points out that even venerated philosophers such as Plato and Aristotle should not be viewed as the only sources of philosophical wisdom:

> Plato and Aristotle are often interesting because they are wicked and wrong; because they provide us with access to worlds of thought that are

alien, stretching our conception of the range of human thought; because we can trace, in tracing the history of reflection on their work, a single fascinating strand in the history of the mental life of our species.[6]

Instead of asking what Black philosophy *is*, especially compared to European philosophy, Appiah reshapes the question: He asks, '[What sorts of *projects*] should philosophers concerned with the intellectual health of the [African] continent pursue?' For an answer, he turns to the highly respected black writer and intellectual Richard Wright:

> (1) The thought of the African people is intrinsically valuable and should be studied for that reason, if for no other; (2) it is important to the history of ideas that we discover and understand the relation between (or influence of) African thought and the thought of the Western world ... And, (3) it is important in understanding practical affairs that we clearly delineate their underlying philosophical motivation.[7]

I think this separation of intellectual labour is a useful approach to understanding how indigenous intellectuals in North America can understand their relationship to European philosophical thought.

For me, though, the problem is not merely about gaining greater access – at least, if by access we mean simply producing greater numbers of indigenous academics. There is a complex relationship between forms of knowledge (and thus indigenous intellectual practices) rooted in indigenous communities and the legal and political practices of the state, and we need to pay closer attention to that complexity. The number of indigenous intellectuals who participate in the intellectual life of the dominant culture is always going to be very small. I contend that *how* we choose to participate matters greatly.

The first difficulty is to know how we ought to characterize the distinct forms of knowledge embedded in indigenous communities. Phrases like 'traditional knowledge' and 'indigenous ways of knowing' have become commonplace in both mainstream and indigenous cultures, yet we are not at all clear about what they mean *in relation to the legal and political discourses of the dominant culture*. Indigenous peoples assert that they have distinct ways of knowing the world. If we are to sustain this claim in the dominant culture, we will have to be clear about what these forms of knowing are, and more importantly, what role they ought to play in asserting and protecting the rights, sovereignty, and nationhood of our communities.

A second difficulty arises when we shift our perspective and look out towards the dominant culture – in particular, to the legal and political practices of the state. Does the formal recognition of Aboriginal rights, sovereignty, and nationhood (meaning recognition *within* existing Canadian legal and political practices) require the direct participation of indigenous ways of knowing? This is not a trivial question: it goes to the core of what I am trying to argue in this book. It seems to me that if we take Kymlicka's constraint seriously, Aboriginal peoples need to be able to use the languages of rights, sovereignty, and nationhood when asserting and defending the legal and political integrity of their communities. The difficulty here is that we are not clear about *how* we are to use indigenous ways of knowing to foster a useful and more inclusive Aboriginal rights discourse in Canada.

Allow me to return to the claim I made in the introduction: *If* Aboriginal peoples want to claim that they possess different world views, and furthermore, if they want to assert that these differences ought to matter politically in the Aboriginal–Canadian state legal and political relationship, *then* they must engage the Canadian state's legal and political discourses in more effective ways. We need to find ways to shape the legal and political relationship so that it respects indigenous world views while generating a useful 'theory' of Aboriginal rights.

But what does it mean to be 'more effective'? White Paper liberalism was offered as a way for Aboriginal peoples to participate more equitably in the day-to-day life of Canadian society, but it is not the kind of participation that Aboriginal peoples are demanding. Aboriginal peoples claim a form of difference that other Canadians do not possess; furthermore, they claim this form of difference necessitates formal legal and political recognition that they have special rights and that these rights ought to be protected by the highest law in the land – the *Canadian Constitution*.

The first indigenous project focuses on the study of indigenous philosophy as an inherently valuable intellectual exercise. Appiah calls this approach to doing philosophy 'ethnophilosophy'; I call it doing 'indigenous philosophy' proper.[8] This kind of activity involves highly specialized forms of thinking; it is a distinctly indigenous activity. The Anishnabi have the Midewewin Lodge (Midé), a society of medicine people who are responsible for preserving Anishnabi philosophy and ceremonies. To become a full member of this lodge one must be of strong moral character (as judged by other medicine people) and undergo years of difficult training and study. All of this learning is done in the Anishnabi language, and all Anishnabi people, although most are not privileged to sit in the Midé, learn from these indigenous philosophers.[9]

An academic example of indigenous philosophy in its published form is *Black Elk Speaks*, by John G. Neihardt, the American non-Indian poet and English professor.[10] Neihardt's translation of the Oglala medicine man's thought is revered by many as a model of American Indian philosophical thought. There are a host of serious (some argue insurmountable) epistemological problems inherent in publishing indigenous philosophy, the most immediate being that indigenous knowledge systems are rooted in oral traditions and expressed in indigenous languages and have only just recently been written down. Also, we have to ask: 'What counts as indigenous philosophy, and how do we articulate its content?' Regardless, indigenous philosophy is meant to focus on indigenous thought 'from the inside,' which means that its content must be situated in an indigenous cultural context.[11]

The first project focuses on indigenous ways of doing philosophy, whereas the second calls for doing European philosophy *as an indigenous person*.[12] In this way it facilitates a cross-cultural dialogue. Just as there are many ways of doing philosophy within academia there are many ways that indigenous peoples can engage the European philosophical tradition. There are Hegelians, Kantians, Habermasians, liberals in various traditions, Heideggerians, Wittgensteinans, and countless others who have found places for themselves in the European philosophical landscape. There is no reason why indigenous peoples cannot find their own places in this landscape; all it takes is training and time. But I am interested in the special situation where an indigenous person doing philosophy makes a difference *politically*. I'm sure that Anishnabi understandings of being can be juxtaposed with Heidegger's concept of *Dasein*, and no doubt some kind of rich *philosophical* dialogue may come out of this inquiry.[13] At this point in the so-called intellectual dialogue with the dominant culture, indigenous intellectuals can certainly set out on these philosophical journeys, but it seems to me that we must first and foremost concentrate our limited academic numbers – and thus our limited intellectual energies – on defending the legal and political status of indigenous nationhood.[14] This leads to the third project.

In the third project, indigenous intellectuals engage European ideas as both a philosophical exercise and a political activity. It is not enough to simply engage European thought on its own terms; indigenous intellectuals need to critically engage European ideas, methodologies, and theories to show how they have marginalized, distorted, and ignored indigenous voices. The difference between the second and third projects is that the third approach makes an investigation of the meaning and praxis of colonialism a central activity of an indigenous intellectual community. The dialogue between indigenous intellectuals and their non-indigenous counterparts created by unpacking colonialism from the history of ideas generates the philosophical battleground for word warriors. This kind of intellectual dialogue can lead us to what I call a 'critical indigenous philosophy.'

One problem with looking at indigenous intellectual projects in this way is that the North American indigenous experience does not map so neatly onto Wright's division of intellectual labour. Let us return to our dilemma: indigenous intellectuals need to ask themselves what it means for them to claim that they have unique ways of understanding the world, and that the differences matter, both legally and politically; at the same time, they must insist on greater participation in what the dominant culture deems to be exclusively non-indigenous intellectual practices. In other words, how do we explain our differences and in the process empower ourselves to actually change the state's legal and political practices? Indigenous peoples have been consistent throughout the five-hundred years since contact when explaining their world views, but far less successful at bringing about change in the Eurocentric philosophical theories and practices of justice. It is one kind of activity to speak or write about indigenous philosophy; it is quite another to weave indigenous thinking into Western philosophical thinking (or vice versa). To complicate matters epistemologically and politically (or at least it ought to complicate matters), any hopes for a rich dialogue must be articulated in the language of the dominant culture. Understanding and articulating indigenous philosophy, whether in oral or written form, is a valuable intellectual project, but we need to be clear about what work it can do for us within the European intellectual community and, more importantly, in contemporary legal and political practices. Allow me to cite an example to clarify this point:

In his recent book *An Indian Mind in a Linear World*, Donald Fixico tries to argue that the American Indian mind thinks in a fundamentally different way from the European mind.[15] He begins his book by stating:

'Indian thinking' is 'seeing' things from a perspective emphasizing that circles and cycles are central to the world and that all things are related within the universe. For Indian people who are close to their tribal traditions and native values, they think within a native reality consisting of a physical and metaphysical world. Full bloods and people raised in the traditional ways of their peoples see things in this combined manner. ... This point of view is a different perspective from that of the American mainstream, based on the Western mind believing in empirical evidence.

By placing concepts in quotations, Fixico is using Western philosophical concepts – 'thinking,' 'seeing,' 'physical world,' 'metaphysical world,' 'empirical evidence,' and so on – to argue that the Indian has a fundamentally different perspective on the world than Europeans. His project, as a *philosophical* exercise, is doomed right from the first sentence of his book.[16] He is using uncritically the language of the dominant intellectual culture to explain the normative content of an indigenous world view, presumably in order to convince mainly nonindigenous readers; concomitantly, he is drawing conclusions about European philosophical thinking without actually 'doing' Western philosophy.

For example, the terms 'physical' and 'metaphysical' worlds are by no means unproblematic in European philosophy; in fact, much of twentieth-century philosophy has been obsessed with avoiding metaphysical language.[17] If Fixico is using these terms to explain what he means by how reality is distinguished in American Indian philosophical thought, then, ironically, he is caricaturing American Indian philosophical thought. Why should Fixico use a term like 'metaphysical' – one of the most contentious and some would argue vaguest concepts in the Western philosophical tradition – to do so much work to explain what he believes is a unique indigenous distinction in American Indian philosophy? It seems to me that there are many indigenous conceptions of reality that can be explained in an ethnophilosophical way – that is, by using an indigenous language to explain the indigenous world view. This is essentially what I mean by 'doing' indigenous philosophy. Fixico does cite several American Indian concepts in his discussion – ones he is no doubt familiar with – but he does not contextualize them deeply enough within an indigenous world for them to make sense to a critical reader (assuming he is trying to convince the reader of something). In other words, he doesn't situate them in their rightful place; rather, he holds them up as objects of comparison – compares them *to* European concepts. This brings us back to Appiah's point about indigenous philosophy gaining its legitimacy through being measured against European philosophy.

But Fixico also caricatures European philosophy. Western European philosophy is, if anything, a critical activity, and to invoke problematic terms like 'metaphysical' and 'reality' without explaining how they are being used is to render one's voice at best unclear and vague, and at worst incoherent. So he is misusing his normative terms in an American Indian philosophical context and is also using them uncritically in a European philosophical context. Fixico believes he is doing indigenous philosophy *and* European philosophy, when in fact, to a critical reader, he is doing neither effectively. He is claiming that American Indian people experience the world differently and that this difference, however we characterize it, matters to Western European philosophy (itself a linear argument!). This claim, however, ought to be the conclusion of an argument, not the starting point of what ought to be a very difficult philosophical exercise (in both indigenous and European philosophy).

The real danger with Fixico's approach is pedagogical. This is because he is implicitly telling young indigenous minds that the problems (especially the associated political problems) of understanding the complex relationship between indigenous ways of thinking about the world and the discourses of European philosophy are, in fact, not complex, but are easily solved without seriously engaging either indigenous or European philosophy. Mind you, he is not clear about whom he is writing for, and by making this clear from the start of his discussion he would go a long way towards shaping his normative language. I should say that I appreciate what Fixico is trying to argue – that there are differences between indigenous and European ways of understanding the world and that they matter, especially to how indigenous people think about themselves – but we need to be very careful about how we defend this view in mainstream academia.[18]

Perhaps a more sophisticated approach is found in the work of the Lumbee legal scholar Robert Williams Jr. His first book, *The American Indian in Western Legal Thought*, is a well-researched account of the history of European legal and political thought.[19] His method is distinctly academic – legal history – and the text has proven very useful for scholars in various fields, from law to literary criticism. Although he discusses the history of European legal and political thought, he places the American Indian at the centre of his research. His study reveals shortcomings in various legal and political theories; more importantly, it shows how European thought contains deeply embedded colonial assumptions about American Indians. He goes back to before first contact to provide some context for explaining why Europeans colonized the New World in the way they did. He attempts to lay out what was meant by the discourses of the papacy, the Crusades, and the various strands of humanism to show how these culminated in legal theories and practices that justified the dispossession of indigenous lands. This, in a sense, is his 'theory' of colonial law, and it can be considered part of the academic field of legal scholarship.

What is interesting about Williams as an indigenous scholar is that his more recent book, *Linking Arms Together: American Indian Treaty Visions of Law and Peace, 1600–1800*, tells a much different story. He states:

> Soon after completing *The American Indian in Western Legal Thought*, I realized the need to imagine a very different kind of work for my next project. I had set out in that first book to tell the history of the legal ideas that the West brought to the New World to justify the colonization of American Indian peoples. But this, as I knew even then, was only half the story. As the cultural critic Edward Said has written, nearly everywhere in the non-Western world, the coming of the white man brought forth a response.[20]

Williams is acutely aware of the problem of the indigenous voice in American legal culture, which makes sense because he teaches the white man's law to mostly white students. In his first book, the American Indian is the *object* of a historical legal analysis; in his second, he brings the American Indian *voice* to the centre of his analysis. Perhaps his two books, taken together, can be seen as an attempt to engage legal scholarship from an indigenous perspective (the second project), while showing how legal thought remains embedded in colonial assumptions about American Indians and their ways of thinking (the third project). How well he accomplishes this *philosophically* remains to be determined by a community of indigenous and non-indigenous legal scholars.

It is this third project that has the potential to empower indigenous intellectuals in mainstream intellectual culture. The second project declares in effect that if indigenous intellectuals are going to participate in European intellectual culture, they better know what they are talking about. For example, if one is going to write about law, then one had better know something about its methodologies and history, about what counts as competent legal reasoning, and about what it takes to become recognized as a member of the legal intellectual community. The third project demands much more of indigenous intellectuals in that it is not enough for them to simply seek membership in the intellectual community of the dominant culture – one has to make the indigenous voice the centre of one's intellectual life. The indigenous intellectual's place in the dominant culture will always be problematic because virtually every aspect of indigenous life remains steeped in colonialism. This is, of course, a controversial claim to make in academia. For most mainstream non-indigenous intellectuals, claims that much of their intellectual tradition remains steeped in colonialism meet with resistance and even hostility; therefore these claims need to be defended at many different levels.[21]

Colonialism is not something that is deeply 'intellectualized' in indigenous communities; it is embedded in the everydayness of indigenous life. Those who have made inroads into mainstream academic life, who have raised their voices against the injustices of the existing political relationship and defended the nationhood of their tribes, have met great resistance. American Indian intellectuals such as Vine Deloria, Elizabeth Cook-Lynn, Beatrice Medicine, and Jack Forbes have been working against mainstream American intellectual culture for more than thirty years.[22] Elizabeth Cook-Lynn, in her article 'Who Stole Native American studies,' examines the evolution of Native American studies programs since their inception in American universities in the late 1960s.[23] She argues that as a discipline, Native American studies should 'center on two concepts: *indigenousness* (culture, place, and philosophy) and *sovereignty* (history and law).'[24] She rails against American academia for failing to allow Native American studies the freedom to create institutional space for American Indian intellectuals to develop 'new epistemologies.' These new epistemologies cannot arise from the traditional disciplines of the social sciences and humanities; rather, 'new epistle writers who understand that the defense of the land and indigenous nationhood is what is at stake must do the work.'[25] For Cook-Lynn, the 'work' that Native intellectuals must undertake is to reflect on our indigenousness – what I have labelled 'indigeneity' – to defend our rights, sovereignty, and nationhood, and to show that colonialism is 'a monstrous crime against humanity.'[26]

But Cook-Lynn does not provide us with the philosophical alternatives from which these new epistemologies are supposed to evolve. Even so, she is right to point out that we must do the 'work'; that is, we Native intellectuals must speak, and think critically for ourselves, and we can only do so effectively from within a rigorous *critical* intellectual environment. This critical environment must engage not only indigenous philosophy but also the methodologies of the social sciences and humanities.[27] Where I differ from Cook-Lynn is that I believe a healthy indigenous intellectual culture must *include* the discourses that have evolved out of the so-called traditional disciplines, many of which have arisen as responses to the oppressive nature of Eurocentric academic disciplines. Cook-Lynn seems to be suggesting that these new epistemologies, whatever they are, can arise independently, or at least with little interaction with the dominant intellectual culture. To a certain extent this may be true, especially if one is doing indigenous philosophy; however, I believe that defending the sovereignty and nationhood of tribal life requires us to aim our intellectual energies towards the dominant culture's peculiar ways of characterizing who we are as human beings, and especially as political entities.[28]

Perhaps I am not so much disagreeing with Cook-Lynn as calling for greater intellectual participation in mainstream academia, although this is not the whole answer to the difficult question of how to generate a rigorous indigenous intellectual culture. If we take seriously the idea that protecting indigenous nationhood is a priority for an indigenous intellectual culture, we need to be able to speak and write convincingly in indigenous terms *and* be able to change how these arguments are used in the institutions of the state. Indigenous intellectuals must be both philosophical *and* political. But how is this possible? I believe part of the answer lies in how well indigenous peoples can reconcile an indigenous academic culture with the existing forms of leadership found in indigenous nations. Thinking about indigenous problems, engaging other people's ideas, publishing one's thoughts, and holding dialogues with those who disagree with us means little if these ideas do not lead to transformations in indigenous nations. Those nations require intellectual leaders and political leaders to work together.

Taiaiake Alfred makes leadership the focus of his work: indigenous forms of governance will never become a reality if they are not guided by traditional indigenous values. Alfred is the director of the School of Indigenous Governance at the University of Victoria, where he works mostly with indigenous students from many nations, many of whom will return to their communities. Alfred, a Mohawk from Kahnawake, is an indigenous nationalist – a Mohawk nationalist to be more precise. This means he sees the indigenous political relationship with the state – at least his own community's – as a relationship between equal nations.[29] He argues throughout his work that the Haudenosaunee have never relinquished their nationhood; in fact, it makes no sense to think they could, because if they did, they would literally no longer exist as Haudenosaunee.

But Alfred's nationalism is also a form of separatism. He defends the view that indigenous peoples possess the unilateral ability to withdraw from the colonial relationship; he does so by embracing a more politically empowering form of indigenous nationalism. This form of political empowerment is possible *only* if indigenous people embrace, or 're'-embrace, their *traditional values*. Alfred views isolationism in a unequivocally positive way: by turning our backs to the colonial state – physically, spiritually, and intellectually – and adopting indigenous traditional forms of governance, we can create healthy indigenous nations.

This 're-turning' by embracing traditional values is the means for what Alfred really wants to implement through his manifesto: indigenous forms of governance. He states early in *Peace, Power, and Righteousness* that his book 'is concerned not with the process through which self-government is negotiated, but with the end goals and the nature of indigenous governments, *once decolonization has been achieved.*'[30] He adds, a few pages later: 'To many of these traditionalists it seems that, so far, all the attention and energy has been directed at the process of decolonization – the mechanics of removing ourselves from direct state control and the legal and political struggle to gain recognition of an indigenous governing authority. Almost no attention has been paid to the end goals of the struggle.'[31] For Alfred, the end goal of our struggle is indigenous forms of governance, and this goal is what ought to drive the political relationship with the dominant culture.

How do we get there? According to Alfred, we get there by rejecting the *values* of the dominant culture and, in many cases by (re)embracing the *values* of our ancestors. At the same time, we commit ourselves to (re)adopting traditional forms of governance. We get there by our leaders breaking away from the colonial political framework (DIAND in Canada, the BIA in the United States) and by purposefully situating and representing indigenous forms of governance as the only legitimate forms of government in the community. This is a courageous stance to take in contemporary Aboriginal politics in Canada, but Alfred is no stranger to showing intellectual courage. He follows in the tradition of Vine Deloria, the venerated Lakota thinker whose writings, while academic in methodology, project a profound anger at Eurocentric ways of thinking about the world. Both Deloria and Alfred are strongly critical of mainstream intellectual culture – especially its forms of governance – and quick to lash out against colonial attitudes, both in writing and in practice.[32]

But they are also critical of indigenous leadership. Contemporary indigenous leaders have become far too dependent on the federal government, to the point that many are unable to assert an authentic political indigenous voice. If indigenous leaders could motivate their people to reject the ways of the colonial culture and to politicize their allegiance to traditional ways, the rest would take care of itself. Traditional forms of leadership are best at asserting and protecting indigenous forms of nationhood – which for Alfred are the only legitimate forms of indigenous government: 'Understanding leadership means understanding indigenous political philosophy: conceptions of power, and the primary values that create legitimacy and allow governments to function appropriately and effectively.'[33] Alfred presents an intriguing argument, especially since he raises three important problems that must be central to a critical indigenous philosophy. I will consider them in turn.

The first problem Alfred relates to is the idea of decolonization. For Alfred, colonialism is a shadowy concept. It is something physical, like a force, and therefore something that can be controlled, manipulated, even eliminated. After a poignant discussion of 'colonial mentalities,' he goes on to add: 'Attempting to decolonize without addressing the structural imperatives of the colonial system itself is clearly futile. Yet most people accept the idea that we are making steady progress toward the resolution of injustices stemming from colonization. Most Native people do not see any need for a massive reorientation of the relationship between themselves and the state. This is symptomatic of the colonial mentality.'[34]

Alfred is right to make colonialism, and decolonization, a political problem for indigenous peoples. But it is not *only* a political problem. What do we mean when we say that colonial mentalities have taken a stranglehold on indigenous communities? In the language of postcolonialism, Alfred tells us that 'the colonial mentality is the intellectual dimension in the group of emotional and psychological pathologies associated with internalized oppression.'[35] Colonialism is embedded in the very being of indigenous life, which for many indigenous peoples includes the spiritual dimension of their existence. It is the *process* of decolonization that I find difficult to imagine. As with the drive for indigenous forms of political recognition, in order to create the space for us to be free from colonialism, we must engage the dominant culture. We may not know what the process will look like, but we do know it has to be a dialogical one.

Colonial discourses, and now postcolonial discourses, may or may not be ultimately useful for indigenous politics, but it seems to me that these forms of intellectual projects work with a view of colonialism that involves a complex, intercultural set of relations that are dynamic in nature. Colonialism has influenced virtually every aspect of indigenous people's daily lives: language, religion, sexuality, art, philosophy, and politics. Alfred is right to point out that colonialism has to end and that indigenous peoples can play a major role in bringing about that end, but we need to know how to go about doing so. Abolishing colonialism is the goal of many indigenous and non-indigenous peoples; finding a way to do it is the great dilemma. If a just political relationship has to be dialogical in nature, indigenous peoples will not be able to secure a 'postcolonial' political relationship without the help of non-indigenous people. But making sense of the meaning of colonialism, and especially addressing colonialism in 'philosophical thinking,' is relatively new territory for indigenous intellectuals.

Second, Alfred commits himself to a normative concept of traditionalism. Colonialism is woven deeply into virtually every aspect of life for indigenous peoples; this means that the idea of traditionalism needs to be recast in the light of how we understand colonialism and indigenous nationalism. The process is once again a dynamic one. Most indigenous peoples know that 'traditional' ways of being exist in contemporary indigenous communities. If we want these ways of being in the world to continue to define our sui generis rights, word warriors will have to protect these forms of knowledge in the academic or European context (one that is published in manifestos). As I have laid out the landscape, three relevant communities are involved in this philosophical and political dialogue: indigenous philosophers, word warriors, and European intellectuals. Word warriors are charged with protecting indigenous philosophies from unjust European philosophical scrutiny. This requires them to acquire knowledge of European philosophy, the history of ideas, and especially their own indigenous philosophies. Weaving together these three strands of intellectual life could produce strong intellectual leadership, which could then be used to guide the legal and political strategies of indigenous politics.[36]

Traditionalism has come to have political significance; in some cases it has become a rarified term that renders indigenous thought immune from criticism. Traditionalism is invoked as a normative bridging term between indigenous philosophies and European intellectual culture. It may be an important concept for indigenous arguments, but we must have some say over how it is used in the legal and political discourses of the state. For many indigenous peoples the concept of traditionalism is closely related to another central (and, I would argue, problematic) concept in indigenous philosophies – indigenous 'spirituality.' I will say more soon about spirituality. For now, I point out that indigenous spirituality is central to indigenous philosophical thinking, which European cultures cannot and will not respect on its own terms.

In a sense, this is *the* most significant difference between indigenous and European world views. As indigenous people, many of us believe we can explain our understandings of the 'spiritual' and that the dominant culture will some day 'get it.' But history has shown us that at least at this time in the relationship, we must keep to ourselves our sacred knowledge as we articulate and understand it from within our own cultures, for it is this knowledge that defines us as indigenous peoples. This 'Crazy Horse' approach to protecting indigenous philosophies is necessary for our survival as indigenous peoples. Yet at the same time, we must continue to assert and protect our rights, sovereignty, and nationhood within an ongoing colonial relationship. This makes the role of word warriors all the more important, and all the more difficult as well, because it strains our relationships with our communities so that we risk being ostracized by both indigenous and mainstream worlds.

Third and finally, Alfred's political thought incorporates a strong form of indigenous nationalism. He rails against the 'rights' approach to defining the political relationship, and I have some sympathy with this; but given that the dominant political community is a constitutional democracy, rights-based approaches are inescapable. The solution to this political problem may lie in shifting the discourse from the language of rights to the language of nationalism, but the fact remains that we must use the legal and political language of the dominant culture in negotiating our legal and political relationships with the state. Mohawk nationalism – at least the way Alfred uses it in the political relationship with the American and Canadian states – is embedded in the political context of the nation-state. The Iroquois may view this form of recognition as empowering – and it probably is, for the Iroquois – but the discourse of nationhood remains very much a discourse of the state. The meaning of nationhood evolves out of the negotiated, ongoing political relationship, and the Iroquois may have some say in shaping that meaning, but the politics of nationhood remain a distinctly Eurocentric practice. This means that the discourse of nationhood may or may not empower Aboriginal communities – it depends on the context of the legal and political relationship. For most indigenous communities in a constitutional democracy, political realities continue to be shaped in terms of rights. Regardless, the problems of explaining colonialism, traditionalism, and nationhood ought to be the work of an indigenous intellectual culture, and we must rely on these understandings as we work to change public policies.

John Borrows's legal scholarship engages Canadian law while developing sophisticated indigenous critiques and methodologies in ways that will, I believe, show positive results in legal and political practices. But Borrows is a very rare indigenous person indeed: he speaks his language, and he is one of a handful of legal experts who understands, teaches, and publishes about Aboriginal law. He is an exemplar of Aboriginal participation – he is a word warrior. His professional life, though, is largely embedded in white culture. His approach to engaging European legal culture – what I would loosely call a methodology – is to juxtapose mainstream legal analyses with specific examples of indigenous legal practices. He refers to, and uses, Aboriginal legal systems, mostly Anishnabi, alongside discussions of the Canadian state's legal system, but in the process he doesn't focus on *what* he is doing. The purpose of his kind of legal analysis is to show that indigenous peoples have their own legal practices and that they are equivalent in moral status to Euro-Canadian practices.

I agree with this claim, but the brutal reality is that the Canadian state's legal and political culture *does not* recognize the moral worth of Aboriginal legal practices – whatever they are – as legitimate alternatives to what is unproblematically recognized as the *only* legitimate legal system in Canada. His legal scholarship sheds light on the problems of reconciling Aboriginal political practices with Euro-Canadian legal and political practices, and the newcomer's unilateral assertions of sovereignty, but it does little to suggest what can be done to change the *attitudes* of the newcomers.

The track record for courts recognizing the legitimacy of Aboriginal ways of knowing is not good – in fact, it is abysmal. Kymlicka's constraint is a reality check that our generation has to live with: for better or worse, the people we have to convince are in most of the positions of power and almost all of them are non-Aboriginal. Most Aboriginal leaders understand that the state's legal and political processes are, in many ways, 'the only game in town.' For Borrows, the number of Aboriginal people with a hand in the legal and political practices of the state needs to increase *because* a greater Aboriginal presence in these practices will empower Aboriginal people, which ultimately will empower Aboriginal communities. This leads to one of the main points of his work: Aboriginal professionals need to make greater inroads into the Canadian legal and political systems.

Like Cairns, Borrows is an optimist, and perhaps that is a good thing, because the alternative to increasing Aboriginal participation lies not in overcoming colonialism or reconciling it with a renewed form of Aboriginal nationalism, but rather in a victory on the part of the state. Borrows does not explain how Aboriginal participation, or 'Aboriginal control of Canadian affairs,' is to evolve in the face of crushing legal defeats like *Van der Peet* and celebrated policy proposals like the *First Nation Governance Act*, except to say that in the end, we must begin to empower Aboriginal people by placing them in positions of greater legal and political influence. There is an implicit assumption that this kind of participation is unquestionably good for Aboriginal peoples because it means they will have a greater say in how policies are designed, drafted, and applied. But as I have been trying to show, it matters *how* indigenous knowledge is brought into courtrooms, political negotiations, and university classrooms.

Alfred and Borrows are good examples of how indigenous voices are finding their way into the mainstream intellectual culture, but they are part of a very small indigenous intellectual culture, and for many non-indigenous scholars their work seems like a footnote to mainstream political science and legal scholarship.[37] Yet we have to evolve with what we have, and intellectuals like Alfred and Borrows give us reason to hope that indigenous intellectuals will be recognized in mainstream academia even while they maintain strong connections to their communities.

Patricia Monture, a Mohawk professor of sociology at the University of Saskatchewan, shows how difficult it is for educated Indians to feel at home in mainstream academia. Monture was a law professor at the University of Ottawa for five years until she finally realized that 'law contains no answers but is in fact a very large and very real part of the problem Aboriginal people continue to face.'[38] She decided to leave her tenured position and move to Saskatchewan. She argues that she is now closer to an Indian intellectual community, although she does not purport to know exactly what that means in terms of her own identity as a so-called educated Indian and of her responsibilities as an Indian mother, teacher, and intellectual leader. For her, indigenous 'independence' involves far more than simple recognition of indigenous peoples as self-determining nations within a constitutional democracy. She eloquently states:

Maintaining good relationships with your family, clan and nation, but the rest of the living world as well (by which I mean the environment and all things around us), means that you are fulfilling one of your basic responsibilities as a human being. It is this web (or the natural laws) that is the relationship that has been devastated by colonialism ... I no longer believe that Canadian law has a role to play in fixing the damage to this web. This of course forced me to do a lot of thinking about where I (and we) can turn our energies in search of solutions.[39]

I do not agree that law does not have a role to play in securing a political relationship that will allow indigenous communities to thrive, but Monture is right to point towards indigenous philosophy as the source of our future well-being as indigenous peoples. Her work highlights another important point about indigenous intellectual communities: we must resolve our own societal problems, and in our own ways, but we cannot do so while we are still held in a legal and political straitjacket by the Canadian state. Her experiences as a law professor show how hostile the dominant intellectual culture can be, but it does not follow from this hostility that indigenous peoples must not participate in these agonic communities. Regardless, Monture has travelled a rough road and continues to be an important and active voice in Canadian indigenous intellectual culture.

Indigenous intellectuals, then – at least those who explicitly engage the legal and political discourses of the state – need to engage in three kinds of overlapping activities. First, they must engage colonialism in its physical and intellectual contexts and in the process strive to overcome the colonial mindset in both indigenous and non-indigenous communities. Second, they must protect and defend our 'indigeneity'; that is, they must work to ensure that indigenous ways of knowing the world are not devalued, marginalized, or ridiculed in the marketplace of ideas. Third and finally, an indigenous intellectual community must assert and defend the integrity of indigenous political rights in the legal and political discourses of the state. This is no easy task, but I see hope in many of the young indigenous and non-indigenous people who seek justice for indigenous peoples.

Still, there is much intellectual work to be done. Alfred, Borrows, and Monture are not philosophers – that is, philosophers trained in the European tradition. Which leads one to ask: What can an indigenous person who *is* trained in European philosophy *do* to play a more effective role in the relationship between the indigenous political leadership,

which finds its roots in indigenous philosophy, and the European intellectual tradition, which is used in articulating the content of Aboriginal
rights discourse in Canada?[40] I believe there are two important roles a
philosopher can play.

The first is pedagogical. From my own experience, I have seen too
many indigenous students come into university resisting the idea that
learning European forms of knowledge, never mind critiquing European ways of thinking, is important for their intellectual development.
Don't get me wrong – there are very good reasons for this resistance,
and I don't think every person, indigenous or non-indigenous, is suited
to this kind of intellectual journey. Indigenous professors are obligated
to guide their students through complex intellectual landscapes so that
they can begin to think for themselves how ideas relate to their
indigeneity. Like all students, indigenous students need to learn bodies
of knowledge in order to be able to think effectively; and if indigenous
students leave university without at least knowing the social, legal, and
political history of the Indian–white relationship, they have failed to
receive a good education and their chances of becoming effective indig--
enous intellectuals are severely limited.

But 'thinking about thinking' is the philosopher's intellectual domain, and indigenous philosophy professors can explicitly weave the
third intellectual project into their teaching. As I stated earlier: indigenous intellectuals engage European ideas both as a *philosophical* exercise and as a *political* activity. It is not enough to simply engage European
thought on its own terms; indigenous intellectuals need to critically
engage European ideas, methodologies, and theories to show how they
have marginalized, distorted, and ignored indigenous voices. In order
to do this effectively, we must first come to understand, *as best we can*,
the European history of ideas *on its own terms*.[41] This means we need
to understand how normative language – that is, the language that
makes substantive claims about 'what is the case' – is put to use in a
particular way of perceiving the world. Once we do understand, we
can assess whether this normative language is useful for us as indigenous intellectuals.

The second role a philosopher *can* play in reconciling the indigenous
and European traditions has to do with addressing a concept I have
tried to avoid in this book: the spiritual dimension of our indigeneity.
From an indigenous perspective, when we think about thinking it is
impossible for us to avoid the centrality of the spiritual in how we
perceive the world. Midé philosophers possess privileged forms of

knowledge, and this knowledge is grounded in profound *spiritual* relationships with the world – how quickly our language becomes muddied! I am indigenous, yet I am *not* an indigenous philosopher; and therefore I ought not to place myself in the privileged position of explaining the *meaning* of indigenous spirituality. In a European philosophical context, having invoked a term like 'spirituality' I must then explain how this normative term is to be used in its rightful place – and do so in the English language. It is this step that can be paralysing. Wittgenstein's famous imperative stops me in my tracks: 'Whereof one cannot speak, thereof one must be silent.'[42]

This does not mean we must ignore the spiritual *dimension* of indigenous thought in our teaching, in our scholarship, or in Canadian courts of law for that matter – far from it. What it does highlight is that when we use a concept like 'spirituality' in European philosophical discourse, especially in political philosophy, we must appreciate that in order for it to do the philosophical work we believe it ought to do – say, in generating a richer understanding of political justice – we must be able to find a place for it within European philosophical discourse. Finding the right 'place' for terms like 'spirituality' is essential to a critical indigenous philosophy.

Eva Marie Garroutte, a Cherokee sociologist, offers what she calls the 'emerging theoretical perspective' of 'Radical Indigenism' as a way of legitimating indigenous philosophies in the academy:

> Stated very simply, Radical Indigenism assumes that scholars can take philosophies of knowledge carried by indigenous peoples seriously. They can consider those philosophies and their assumptions, values, and goals not simply as interesting objects of study (claims that some *believe* to be true) but as intellectual orientations that map out ways of discovering things about the world (claims that, to one degree or another, *reflect* or *engage* the true).

Later she adds:

> Radical Indigenism is centered on the assumption that American Indian (and other indigenous) philosophies of knowledge are rational, articulable, coherent logics for ordering and knowing the world. It pushes beyond that assumption to argue that indigenous philosophies of knowledge, and the models of inquiry they imply, have a place in the academy. This position invites an understanding of these philosophies not merely as

objects of curiosity (unusual things that people have believed) but as tools
for the discovery and generation of knowledge.[43]

One of the main purposes of Garroutte's Radical Indigenism is to
legitimate indigenous ways of knowing the world in the academy, but
we have very different ideas about how this is supposed to occur.
Garroutte is much more optimistic about the future of research in
Indian Country than I am, and she assumes, as a matter of principle,
that it is indeed possible to embrace indigenous ways of knowing the
world and make them, not only understood in the dominant culture,
but recognized as legitimate sources of knowledge about the world. I
contend that it isn't indigenous philosophies of knowledge that must be
taken seriously, but the meaning and praxis of colonialism and its
devastating effects in Indian Country. It is one kind of activity to come
to understand indigenous philosophies on their own terms; it is quite
another to recognize the legitimacy of indigenous philosophies when
they purport to defend strong forms of indigenous rights, sovereignty,
and nationhood.

Indigenous intellectuals must, however, embrace Radical Indigenism
in a thinner form. That is, they must embrace the idea that if we are to
continue to assert and defend the rights, sovereignty, and nationhood
we believe we possess, we must defend the position that indigenous
philosophies of knowledge are rational and coherent. Whether indigenous philosophies are articulable in English remains to be seen. We can
invoke terms like kinship, spirituality, and 'Original Instructions' all we
want, but they will do little political work for us as long as the discourses of rights, sovereignty, and nationhood remain inextricably embedded in the philosophical, ideological, religious, social, and economic
realities of the dominant colonial culture.

A *critical* indigenous philosophy is meant to engage European philosophy while at the same time unpacking the meaning and praxis of
colonialism in the history of ideas. In other words, a critical indigenous
philosophical community requires the voices of indigenous philosophers *and* indigenous intellectuals. This situates word warriors in a
distinctly indigenous intellectual culture that engages European philosophy. Once we understand better the praxis associated with this
division of intellectual labour, we will be better positioned to assert and
defend indigenous peoples' rights, sovereignty, and nationhood in mainstream intellectual culture.

But there are serious problems with the idea of a word warrior, both philosophical and practical. First, how does a word warrior 'philosophically move' between worlds? If the differences are deep, and perhaps ultimately cannot be bridged, how can such a person authentically participate in both worlds? In other words, *what* is at stake when it is claimed there are differences and that they matter in the legal and political relationship? Studying European philosophy may or may not help one articulate and understand these differences, but 'thinking about thinking' can be a complex, anxiety-provoking process, and its effects on one's identity can be profound. Studying philosophy is not like learning a mundane skill; it can change one's way of being in the world, and one is not immune from this kind of change simply because one is indigenous – it depends on how seriously one engages *philosophy*.

For an indigenous person, the problem of assimilation is always close at hand. The anxiety generated by moving between intellectual cultures is real, and many indigenous intellectuals find it easier to become part of mainstream culture. This kind of assimilation will always exist, and it may not always be a bad thing for indigenous peoples as a whole. It becomes dangerous when indigenous intellectuals become subsumed or appropriated by the dominant culture yet continue to act as if they were word warriors. To make matters worse, because our numbers are so small, and the dominant culture may not know who these people are, many of these indigenous intellectuals become institutionally empowered to perpetuate the intellectual colonization of legitimate indigenous thought. Word warriors retain strong connections to their communities, and these connections can manifest themselves in many ways; for example, a competent indigenous tax lawyer can be an important word warrior for many indigenous communities.

The problem of authenticity, of who can speak for whom in an indigenous intellectual culture, is no doubt a thorny one – but it is our problem to discuss and solve! Determining what we can and cannot talk about goes a long way towards resolving the authenticity problem, but I suspect this problem will never go away. My hopes lie not in my own work (as I am only, at best, a guide to intellectual landscapes), but in the intellectual work of future indigenous intellectuals. By showing our young minds that they can participate as intellectual equals in the world without giving up who they are as indigenous peoples, we will empower ourselves to some day return our ways of knowing the world to their rightful place in the landscape of human ideas.

It is these indigenous philosophers who will become our new Pipe Carriers.

Conclusion

White Paper liberalism was the starting point of my discussion, the purpose of which has been to point out the ways many Canadians misunderstand Aboriginal peoples' place in Canadian society. Of the four shortcomings to White Paper liberalism that I have cited, two are especially important. First, is the idea that we cannot hope to generate a rich *philosophical* understanding of Aboriginal rights in Canada without the participation of Aboriginal voices. Second, is the legal and political claim that the legitimacy of the initial formation of the Canadian state is not without controversy. I then cited Cairns and Kymlicka as examples of attempts to 'improve' White Paper liberalism, which in some ways they do. They both recognize that colonialism has been especially destructive and unjust and that Aboriginal peoples are entitled to some form of special recognition, although they differ as to the legal and political significance of this special recognition. I show that despite this 'improvement,' their views fail to listen to indigenous philosophies, and that they do not seriously question the legitimacy of the Canadian state.

Kymlicka does raise what I take to be the central problem in the contemporary legal and political relationship. In fact, the key to understanding my project is to appreciate the significance of what I have called 'Kymlicka's constraint.' Allow me quote it in full (yet again):

> For better or worse, it is predominantly non-Aboriginal judges and politicians who have the ultimate power to protect and enforce Aboriginal rights, and so it is important to find a justification of them that such people can recognize and understand. Aboriginal people have their own understanding of self-government drawn from their own experience, and that is important. But it is also important, politically, to know how non-Aboriginal Canadians – Supreme Court Justices, for example – will understand Aboriginal rights and relate them to their own experiences and traditions ... On the standard interpretation of liberalism, Aboriginal rights are viewed as matters of discrimination and/or privilege, not of equality. They will always, therefore, be viewed with the kind of suspicion that led liberals like Trudeau to advocate their abolition. Aboriginal rights, at least in their robust form, will only be secure when they are viewed, not as competing with liberalism, but as an essential component of liberal political practice.[44]

The purpose of this book is not to save liberalism, but to point out that Kymlicka's constraint creates a serious philosophical and political problem for an indigenous intellectual community. It generates a tension between the forms of knowledge that are embedded in Aboriginal communities and the legal and political discourses of the state – discourses that are used to express the meaning and content of Aboriginal rights, sovereignty, and nationhood.

I have called for a division of intellectual labour that essentially delineates two kinds of intellectual leaders. First, there are indigenous philosophers. These people are central to the future survival of indigenous communities *as distinct peoples* because without indigenous philosophies we lose our languages, our ceremonies, and our unique ways of understanding the world. Without indigenous philosophies, our 'indigeneity' would lose its significance in our relationship with the dominant culture. The legal and political status of indigenous peoples might continue to exist; but with regard to the survival of indigenous cultures, too much would be lost. No doubt, this implies a kind of indigenous essentialism. Absolutely. Remember, we indigenous people assert that the source of our indigeneity reveals profoundly different ways of understanding the world. Whether these ways can be explained to the dominant culture, and understood by it, or at the very least respected as legitimate, remains to be seen. All I am saying is that at this point in the history of the relationship, indigenous peoples must realize that in the end only indigenous peoples can protect their ways of knowing the world. Indigenous philosophies, then, are essential practices for preserving our indigeneity.

The second kind of indigenous intellectual – the word warrior – is an indigenous person who has been educated in the legal and political discourses of the dominant culture. The primary responsibility of word warriors is to be intimately familiar with the legal and political discourses of the state *while remaining citizens of indigenous nations*. Because their actions in the world have repercussions in their communities, they need to be accountable to their people. Word warriors function in the secular world of global politics and ideas, yet their actions are guided by both indigenous and non-indigenous ways of understanding the world.

Word warriors occupy a strange and often hostile place. They need to secure intellectual allies, participate in the larger intellectual marketplace of human ideas, and influence the legal and political practices that are used to define indigenous rights, sovereignty, and nationhood. Their connections with their communities make them unique as intellectuals. That said, they cannot do their job alone. There are many non-indigenous intellectuals who can help indigenous peoples make their arguments count. Indigenous peoples need some of their own people to engage the European history of ideas; in just the same way, the dominant culture needs some of its own people to listen and learn from indigenous philosophies. Through the evolution of these overlapping intellectual practices, Kymlicka's constraint can become less oppressive to indigenous ways of thinking about the world.

Kymlicka's constraint will not disappear entirely; rather, it will become less relevant once a vigorous intellectual culture allows indigenous voices to help determine the normative language used for defining the meaning and content of Aboriginal rights discourse. The difficult relationship – and the one I flag as central for an indigenous intellectual community – is the relationship between word warriors and indigenous philosophers. Each has a responsibility for a specific intellectual domain, yet they must interact with each other. Word warriors must know what they can and cannot say in the dominant culture; at the same time, indigenous peoples' survival as distinct political entities requires that indigenous philosophers listen to what word warriors have to say about the meaning and content of Aboriginal rights, sovereignty, and nationhood as they are understood and applied in Canadian legal and political practices. Of course, there has always been a relationship between indigenous philosophers and their people; what I am calling for is for a particular kind of synergy between clearly defined intellectual roles. I do not pretend to know whether this division of labour will ultimately empower indigenous forms of governance. The problem I have addressed in this discussion has focused on the oppressive nature of Kymlicka's constraint; at the same time, I have tried to protect the integrity of indigenous ways of thinking about the world.

The main purpose of examining liberalism is not to dismiss it, but rather to show that Aboriginal rights as they are captured in the White Paper, Cairns's Citizens Plus view, and Kymlicka's minority rights view do not allow for the participation of indigenous voices in the normative practices that characterize the meaning and content of Aboriginal rights. But – 'Is Aboriginal participation *required* in order to develop a just account of Aboriginal rights in Canada?' What if Aboriginal peoples are simply wrong in their understanding that rights, sovereignty, and nationhood are required in order to generate useful meanings of, say, section 35(1)?

My response is largely pragmatic. Aboriginal peoples *are* embedded in the ongoing legal and political relationship – they have a normative place in the social and political fabric of Canadian society. This place is guaranteed by section 35(1) of the *Canadian Constitution*. Canadian society prides itself on being a progressive democratic society; this demands that Aboriginal peoples be included in the dialogue over the meaning of their rights. It does not *guarantee* that Aboriginal understandings will dictate the meaning and content of Aboriginal rights; what it does is broaden the intellectual landscape from which the normative language of rights can evolve. Empowering Aboriginal voices in the dialogue that determines the normative language of Aboriginal rights, sovereignty, and nationhood is a *way* of making Kymlicka's constraint less relevant to the political relationship. I believe this kind of accommodation embraces a more mature form of democratic practice than the way we currently understand the Aboriginal–Canadian state relationship.

It is my hope that this form of democratic dialogue will lead us to celebrate, once again, the passing of the pipe.

Appendix: Statement of the Government of Canada on Indian Policy, 1969

Published under the authority of the Honourable Jean Chrétien, PC, MP, Minister of Indian Affairs and Northern Development
Ottawa, 1969
Queen's Printer Cat. No. R32-2469

Introduction

To be an Indian is to be a man, with all a man's needs and abilities. To be an Indian is also to be different. It is to speak different languages, draw different pictures, tell different tales and to rely on a set of values developed in a different world.

Canada is richer for its Indian component, although there have been times when diversity seemed of little value to many Canadians.

But to be a Canadian Indian today is to be someone different in another way. It is to be someone apart – apart in law apart in the provision of government services and, too often, apart in social contacts.

To be an Indian is to lack power – the power to act as owner of your lands, the power to spend your own money and, too often, the power to change your own condition.

Not always, but too often, to be an Indian, is to be without – without a job, a good house, or running water; without knowledge, training or technical skill and, above all, without those feelings of dignity and self-confidence that a man must have if he is to walk with his head held high.

All these conditions of the Indians are the product of history and have nothing to do with their abilities and capacities. Indian relations with other Canadians began with special treatment by government and society, and special treatment has been the rule since Europeans first settled in Canada. Special treatment has made of the Indians a community disadvantaged and apart.

Obviously, the course of history must be changed.

To be an Indian must be to be free – free to develop Indian cultures in an environment of legal, social and economic equality with other Canadians.

Foreword

The Government believes that its policies must lead to the full, free and non-discriminatory participation of the Indian people in Canadian society. Such a goal requires a break with the past. It requires that the Indian people's roles of dependence be replaced by a role of equal status, opportunity and responsibility, a role they can share with all other Canadians.

This proposal is a recognition of the necessity made plain in a year's intensive discussions with Indian people throughout Canada. The Government believes that to continue its past course of action would not serve the interests of either the Indian people or their fellow Canadians.

The policies proposed recognize the simple reality that the separate legal status of Indians and the policies which have flowed from it have kept the Indian people apart from and behind other Canadians. The Indian people have not been full citizens of the communities and provinces in which they live and have not enjoyed the equality and benefits that such participation offers.

The treatment resulting from their different status has been often worse, sometimes equal and occasionally better than that accorded to their fellow citizens. What matters is that it has been different.

Many Indians, both in isolated communities and in cities, suffer from poverty. The discrimination which affects the poor, Indian and non-Indian alike, when compounded with a legal status that sets the Indian apart, provides dangerously fertile ground for social and cultural discrimination.

In recent years there has been a rapid increase in the Indian population. Their health and education levels have improved. There has been a corresponding rise in expectations that the structure of separate treatment cannot meet.

A forceful and articulate Indian leadership has developed to express the aspirations and needs of the Indian community. Given the opportunity, the Indian people can realize an immense human and cultural potential that will enhance their own well-being, that of the regions in which they live and of Canada as a whole. Faced with a continuation of past policies, they will unite only in a common frustration.

The Government does not wish to perpetuate policies which carry with them the seeds of disharmony and disunity, policies which prevent Canadians from fulfilling themselves and contributing to their society. It seeks a partnership to achieve a better goal. The partners in this search are the Indian people, the governments of the provinces, the Canadian community as a whole and the Government of Canada. As all partnerships do, this will require consultation, negotiation, give and take, and co-operation if it is to succeed.

Many years will be needed. Some efforts may fail, but learning comes from failure and from what is learned success may follow. All the partners have to learn; all will have to change many attitudes.

Governments can set examples, but they cannot change the hearts of men. Canadians, Indians and non-Indians alike stand at the crossroads. For Canadian society the issue is whether a growing element of its population will become full participants contributing in a positive way to the general well-being or whether, conversely, the present social and economic gap will lead to their increasing frustration and isolation, a threat to the general well-being of society. For many Indian people, one road does exist, the only road that has existed since Confederation and before, the road of different status, a road which has led to a blind alley of deprivation and frustration. This road, because it is a separate road, cannot lead to full participation, to equality in practice as well as in theory. In the pages which follow, the Government has outlined a number of measures and a policy which it is convinced will offer another road for Indians, a road that would lead gradually away from different status to full social, economic and political participation in Canadian life. This is the choice.

Indian people must be persuaded, must persuade themselves, that this path will lead them to a fuller and richer life. Canadian society as a whole will have to recognize the need for changed attitudes and a truly open society. Canadians should recognize the dangers of failing to strike down the barriers which frustrate Indian people. If Indian people are to become full members of Canadian society they must be warmly welcomed by that society.

The Government commends this policy for the consideration of all Canadians, Indians and non-Indians, and all governments in Canada.

Summary

1 Background

The Government has reviewed its programs for Indians and has considered the effects of them on the present situation of the Indian people. The review has drawn on extensive consultations with the

Indian people, and on the knowledge and experience of many people both in and out of government.

This review was a response to things said by the Indian people at the consultation meetings which began a year ago and culminated in a meeting in Ottawa in April.

This review has shown that this is the right time to change long-standing policies. The Indian people have shown their determination that present conditions shall not persist.

Opportunities are present today in Canadian society and new directions are open. The Government believes that Indian people must not be shut out of Canadian life and must share equally in these opportunities.

The Government could press on with the policy of fostering further education; could go ahead with physical improvement programs now operating in reserve communities; could press forward in the directions of recent years, and eventually many of the problems would be solved. But progress would be too slow. The change in Canadian society in recent years has been too great and continues too rapidly for this to be the answer. Something more is needed. We can no longer perpetuate the separation of Canadians. Now is the time to change.

This Government believes in equality. It believes that all men and women have equal rights. It is determined that all shall be treated fairly and that no one shall be shut out of Canadian life, and especially that no one shall be shut out because of his race.

This belief is the basis for the Government's determination to open the doors of opportunity to *all* Canadians, to remove the barriers which impede the development of people, of regions and of the country.

Only a policy based on this belief can enable the Indian people to realize their needs and aspirations.

The Indian people are entitled to such a policy. They are entitled to an equality which preserves and enriches Indian identity and distinction; an equality which stresses Indian participation in its creation and which manifests itself in all aspects of Indian life.

The goals of the Indian people cannot be set by others; they must spring from the Indian community itself – but government can create a framework within which all persons and groups can seek their own goals.

2 *The New Policy*

True equality presupposes that the Indian people have the right to full and equal participation in the cultural, social, economic and political life of Canada.

The government believes that the framework within which individual Indians and bands could achieve full participation requires:

1. that the legislative and constitutional bases of discrimination be removed;
2. that there be positive recognition by everyone of the unique contribution of Indian culture to Canadian life;
3. that services come through the same channels and from the same government agencies for all Canadians;
4. that those who are furthest behind be helped most;
5. that lawful obligations be recognized;
6. that control of Indians lands be transferred to the Indian people.

The Government would be prepared to take the following steps to create this framework:

1. Propose to Parliament that the Indian Act be repealed and take such legislative steps as may be necessary to enable Indians to control Indian lands and to acquire title to them.
2. Propose to the governments of the provinces that they take over the same responsibility for Indians that they have for other citizens in their provinces. The take-over would be accompanied by the transfer to the provinces of federal funds normally provided for Indian programs, augmented as may be necessary.
3. Make substantial funds available for Indian economic development as an interim measure.
4. Wind up that part of the Department of Indian Affairs and Northern Development which deals with Indian Affairs. The residual responsibilities of the Federal Government for programs in the field of Indian affairs would be transferred to other appropriate federal departments.

In addition, the Government will appoint a Commissioner to consult with the Indians and to study and recommend acceptable procedures for the adjudication of claims.

The new policy looks to a better future for all Indian people wherever they may be. The measures for implementation are straightforward. They require discussion, consultation and negotiation with the Indian people – individuals, bands and associations and with provincial governments.

Success will depend upon the co-operation and assistance of the

Indians and the provinces. The Government seeks this cooperation and will respond when it is offered.

3 *The Immediate Steps*

Some changes could take place quickly. Others would take longer. It is expected that within five years the Department of Indian Affairs and Northern Development would cease to operate in the field of Indian affairs; the new laws would be in effect and existing programs would have been devolved. The Indian lands would require special attention for some time. The process of transferring control to the Indian people would be under continuous review.

The Government believes this is a policy which is just and necessary. It can only be successful if it has the support of the Indian people, the provinces, and all Canadians.

The policy promises all Indian people a new opportunity to expand and develop their identity within the framework of a Canadian society which offers them the rewards and responsibilities of participation, the benefits of involvement and the pride of belonging.

Historical Background

The weight of history affects us all, but it presses most heavily on the Indian people. Because of history, Indians today are the subject of legal discrimination; they have grievances because of past undertakings that have been broken or misunderstood; they do not have full control of their lands; and a higher proportion of Indians than other Canadians suffer poverty in all its debilitating forms. Because of history too, Indians look to a special department of the Federal Government for many of the services that other Canadians get from provincial or local governments.

This burden of separation has its origin deep in Canada's past and in early French and British colonial policy. The elements which grew to weigh so heavily were deeply entrenched at the time of Confederation.

Before that time there had evolved a policy of entering into agreements with the Indians, of encouraging them to settle on reserves held by the Crown for their use and benefit, and of dealing with Indian lands through a separate organization – a policy of treating Indian people as a race apart.

After Confederation, these well-established precedents were followed and expanded. Exclusive legislative authority was given the Parliament of Canada in relation to 'Indians, and Lands reserved for the Indians' under Head 24 of Section 91 of the British North America Act. Special legislation – an Indian Act – was passed, new treaties were entered into, and a network of administrative offices spread across the country either in advance of or along with the tide of settlement.

This system – special legislation, a special land system and separate administration for the Indian people – continues to be the basis of present Indian policy. It has saved for the Indian people places they can call home, but has carried with it serious human and physical as well as administrative disabilities.

Because the system was in the hands of the Federal Government, the Indians did not participate in the growth of provincial and local services. They were not required to participate in the development of their own communities which were tax exempt. The result was that the Indians, persuaded that property taxes were an unnecessary element in their lives, did not develop services for themselves. For many years such simple and limited services as were required to sustain life were provided through a network of Indian agencies reflecting the authoritarian tradition of a colonial administration, and until recently these agencies had staff and funds to do little more than meet the most severe cases of hardship and distress.

The tradition of federal responsibility for Indian matters inhibited the development of a proper relationship between the provinces and the Indian people as citizens. Most provinces, faced with their own problems of growth and change, left the responsibility for their Indian residents to the Federal Government. Indeed, successive Federal Governments did little to change the pattern. The result was that Indians were the almost exclusive concern of one agency of the Federal Government for nearly a century.

For a long time the problems of physical, legal and administrative separation attracted little attention. The Indian people were scattered in small groups across the country, often in remote areas. When they were in contact with the new settlers, there was little difference between the living standards of the two groups.

Initially, settlers as well as Indians depended on game, fish and fur. The settlers, however, were more concerned with clearing land and establishing themselves and differences soon began to appear.

With the technological change of the twentieth century, society became increasingly industrial and complex, and the separateness of the Indian people became more evident. Most Canadians moved to the growing cities, but the Indians remained largely a rural people, lacking both education and opportunity. The land was being developed rapidly, but many reserves were located in places where little development was possible. Reserves were usually excluded from development and many began to stand out as islands of poverty. The policy of separation had become a burden.

The legal and administrative discrimination in the treatment of Indian people has not given them an equal chance of success. It has exposed them to discrimination in the broadest and worst sense of the term – a discrimination that has profoundly affected their confidence that success can be theirs. Discrimination breeds discrimination by example, and the separateness of Indian people has affected the attitudes of other Canadians towards them.

The system of separate legislation and administration has also separated people of Indian ancestry into three groups – registered Indians, who are further divided into those who are under treaty and those who are not; enfranchised Indians who lost, or voluntarily relinquished, their legal status as Indians; and the Métis, who are of Indian ancestry but never had the status of registered Indians.

The Case for the New Policy

In the past ten years or so, there have been important improvements in education, health, housing, welfare and community development. Developments in leadership among the Indian communities have become increasingly evident. Indian people have begun to forge a new unity. The Government believes progress can come from these developments but only if they are met by new responses. The proposed policy is a new response.

The policy rests upon the fundamental right of Indian people to full and equal participation in the cultural, social, economic and political life of Canada.

To argue against this right is to argue *for* discrimination, isolation and separation. No Canadian should be excluded from participation in community life, and none should expect to withdraw and still enjoy the benefits that flow to those who participate.

1 *The Legal Structure*

Legislative and constitutional bases of discrimination must be removed.

Canada cannot seek the just society and keep discriminatory legislation on its statute books. The Government believes this to be self-evident. The ultimate aim of removing the specific references to Indians from the constitution may take some time, but it is a goal to be kept constantly in view. In the meantime, barriers created by special legislation can generally be struck down.

Under the authority of Head 24, Section 91 of the British North America Act, the Parliament of Canada has enacted the Indian Act. Various federal-provincial agreements and some other statutes also affect Indian policies.

In the long term, removal of the reference in the constitution would be necessary to end the legal distinction between Indians and other Canadians. In the short term, repeal of the Indian Act and enactment of transitional legislation to ensure the orderly management of Indian land would do much to mitigate the problem.

The ultimate goal could not be achieved quickly, for it requires a change in the economic circumstances of the Indian people and much preliminary adjustment with provincial authorities. Until the Indian people are satisfied that their land holdings are solely within their control, there may have to be some special legislation for Indian lands.

2 The Indian Cultural Heritage

There must be positive recognition by everyone of the unique contribution of Indian culture to Canadian society.

It is important that Canadians recognize and give credit to the Indian contribution. It manifests itself in many ways; yet it goes largely unrecognized and unacknowledged. Without recognition by others it is not easy to be proud.

All of us seek a basis for pride in our own lives, in those of our families and of our ancestors. Man needs such pride to sustain him in the inevitable hour of discouragement, in the moment when he faces obstacles, whenever life seems turned against him. Everyone has such moments. We manifest our pride in many ways, but always it supports and sustains us. The legitimate pride of the Indian people has been crushed too many times by too many of their fellow Canadians.

The principle of equality and all that goes with it demands that all of us recognize each other's cultural heritage as a source of personal strength.

Canada has changed greatly since the first Indian Act was passed. Today it is made up of many people with many cultures. Each has its own manner of relating to the other; each makes its own adjustments to the larger society.

Successful adjustment requires that the larger groups accept every group with its distinctive traits without prejudice, and that all groups share equitably in the material and non-material wealth of the country.

For many years Canadians believed the Indian people had but two choices: they could be assimilated and lose their Indian identity. Today Canada has more to offer. There is a third choice – a full role in Canadian society and in the economy while retaining, strengthening and developing an Indian identity which preserves the good things of the past and helps Indian people to prosper and thrive.

This choice offers great hope for the Indian people. It offers great opportunity for Canadians to demonstrate that in our open society there is room for the development of people who preserve their different cultures and take pride in their diversity.

This new opportunity to enrich Canadian life is central to the Government's new policy. If the policy is to be successful, the Indian people must be in a position to play a full role in Canada's diversified society, a role which stresses the value of their experience and the possibilities of the future.

The Indian contribution to North American society is often overlooked, even by the Indian people themselves. Their history and tradition can be a rich source of pride, but are not sufficiently known and recognized. Too often, the art forms which express the past are preserved, but are inaccessible to most Indian people. This richness can be shared by all Canadians. Indian people must be helped to become aware of their history and heritage in all its forms, and this heritage must be brought before *all* Canadians in all its rich diversity.

Indian culture also lives through Indian speech and thought. The Indian languages are unique and valuable assets. Recognizing their value is not a matter of preserving ancient ways as fossils, but of ensuring the continuity of a people by encouraging and assisting them to work at the continuing development of their inheritance in the context of the present-day world. Culture lives and develops in the daily life of people, in their communities and in their other associations, and the Indian culture can be preserved, perpetuated and developed only by the Indian people themselves.

The Indian people have often been made to feel that their culture and history are not worthwhile. To lose a sense of worthiness is damaging. Success in life, in adapting to change, and in developing appropriate relations within the community as well as in relation to a wider world, requires a strong sense of personal worth – a real sense of identity.

Rich in folklore, in art forms and in concepts of community life, the Indian cultural heritage can grow and expand further to enrich the general society. Such a development is essential if the Indian people are again to establish a meaningful sense of identity and purpose and if Canada is to realize its maximum potential.

The Government recognizes that people of Indian ancestry must be helped in new ways in this task. It proposes, through the Secretary of State, to support associations and groups in developing a greater appreciation of their cultural heritage. It wants to foster adequate communication among all people of Indian descent and between them and the Canadian community as a whole.

Steps will be taken to enlist the support of Canadians generally. The provincial governments will be approached to support this goal through their many agencies operating in the field. Provincial educational authorities will be urged to intensify their review of school curriculae and course content with a view to ensuring that they adequately reflect Indian culture and Indian contributions to Canadian development.

3 Programs and Services

Services must come through the same channels and from the same government agencies for all Canadians.

This is an undeniable part of equality. It has been shown many times that separation of people follows from separate services. There can be no argument about the principle of common services. It is right.

It cannot be accepted now that Indians should be constitutionally excluded from the right to be treated within their province as full and equal citizens, with all the responsibilities and all the privileges that this might entail. It is in the provincial sphere where social remedies are structured and applied, and the Indian people, by and large, have been non-participating members of provincial society.

Canadians receive a wide range of services through provincial and local governments, but the Indian people and their communities are mostly outside that framework. It is no longer acceptable that the Indian people should be outside and apart. The Government believes that services should be available on an equitable basis, except for temporary differentiation based on need. Services ought not to flow from separate agencies established to serve particular groups, especially not to groups that are identified ethnically.

Separate but equal services do not provide truly equal treatment.

Treatment has not been equal in the case of Indians and their communities. Many services require a wide range of facilities which cannot be duplicated by separate agencies. Others must be integral to the complex systems of community and regional life and cannot be matched on a small scale.

The Government is therefore convinced that the traditional method of providing separate services to Indians must be ended. All Indians should have access to all programs and services of all levels of government equally with other Canadians.

The Government proposes to negotiate with the provinces and conclude agreements under which Indian people would participate in and be served by the full programs of the provincial and local systems. Equitable financial arrangements would be sought to ensure that services could be provided in full measure commensurate with needs. The negotiations must seek agreements to end discrimination while ensuring that no harm is inadvertently done to Indian interests. The Government further proposes that federal disbursements for Indian programs in each province be transferred to that province. Subject to negotiations with the provinces, such provisions would as a matter of principle eventually decline, the provinces ultimately assuming the same responsibility for services to Indian residents as they do for services to others.

At the same time, the Government proposes to transfer all remaining federal responsibilities for Indians from the Department of Indian Affairs and Northern Development to other departments, including the Departments of Regional Economic Expansion, Secretary of State, and Manpower and Immigration.

It is important that such transfers take place without disrupting services and that special arrangements not be compromised while they are subject to consultation and negotiation. The Government will pay particular attention to this.

4 Enriched Services

Those who are furthest behind must be helped most.

There can be little argument that conditions for many Indian people are not satisfactory to them and are not acceptable to others. There can be little question that special services, and especially enriched services, will be needed for some time.

Equality before the law and in programs and services does not necessarily result in equality in social and economic conditions. For that reason, existing programs will be reviewed. The Department of Regional Economic Expansion, the Department of Manpower and Immigration, and other federal departments involved would be prepared to evolve programs that would help break past patterns of deprivation.

Additional funds would be available from a number of different sources. In an atmosphere of greater freedom, those who are able to do so would be expected to help themselves, so more funds would be available to help those who really need it. The transfer of Indian lands to Indian control should enable many individuals and groups to move ahead on their own initiative. This in turn would free funds for further enrichment of programs to help those who are furthest behind. By ending some programs and replacing them with others evolved within the community, a more effective use of funds would be achieved. Administrative savings would result from the elimination of separate agencies as various levels of government bring general programs and resources to bear. By broadening the base of service agencies, this enrichment could be extended to all who need it. By involving more agencies working at different levels, and by providing those agencies with the means to make them more effective, the Government believes that root problems could be attacked, that solutions could be found that hitherto evaded the best efforts and best-directed of programs.

The economic base for many Indians is their reserve land, but the development of reserves has lagged.

Among the many factors that determine economic growth of reserves, their location and size are particularly important. There are a number of reserves located within or near growing industrial areas which could provide substantial employment and income to their owners if they were properly developed. There are other reserves in agricultural areas which could provide a livelihood for a larger number of family units than is presently the case. The majority of the reserves, however, are located in the boreal or wooded regions of Canada, most of them geographically isolated and many having little economic potential. In these areas, low income, unemployment and under-employment are characteristic of Indians and non-Indians alike.

Even where reserves have economic potential, the Indians have been handicapped. Private investors have been reluctant to supply capital for projects on land which cannot be pledged as security. Adequate social and risk capital has not been available from public sources. Most Indians have not had the opportunity to acquire managerial experience, nor have they been offered sufficient technical assistance.

The Government believes that the Indian people should have the opportunity to develop the resources of their reserves so they may contribute to their own well-being and the economy of the nation. To develop Indian reserves to the level of the regions in which they are located will require considerable capital over a period of some years, as well as the provision of managerial and technical advice. Thus the Government believes that all programs and advisory services of the federal and provincial governments should be made readily available to Indians.

In addition, and as an interim measure, the Government proposes to make substantial additional funds available for investment in the economic progress of the Indian people. This would overcome the barriers to early development of Indian lands and resources, help bring Indians into a closer working relationship with the business community, help finance their adjustment to new employment opportunities, and facilitate access to normal financial sources.

Even if the resources of Indian reserves are fully utilized, however, they cannot all properly support their present Indian populations, much less the populations of the future. Many Indians will, as they are now doing, seek employment elsewhere as a means of solving their economic problems. Jobs are vital and the Government intends that the full counseling, occupational training and placement resources of the Department of Manpower and Immigration are used to further employment opportunities for Indians. The government will encourage private employers to provide opportunities for the Indian people.

In many situations, the problems of Indians are similar to those faced by their non-Indian neighbours. Solutions to their problems cannot be found in isolation but must be sought within the context of regional development plans involving all the people. The consequence of an integrated regional approach is that all levels of government – federal, provincial and local – and the people themselves are involved. Helping overcome regional disparities in the economic well-being of Canadians is the main task assigned to the Department of Regional Economic Expansion. The Government believes that the needs of Indian communities should be met within this framework.

5 Claims and Treaties

Lawful obligations must be recognized.

Many of the Indian people feel that successive governments have not dealt with them as fairly as they should. They believe that lands have been taken from them in an improper manner, or without adequate compensation, that their funds have been improperly administered, that their treaty rights have been breached. Their sense of grievance influences their relations with governments and the community and limits their participation in Canadian life.

Many Indians look upon their treaties as the source of their rights to land, to hunting and fishing privileges, and to other benefits. Some believe the treaties should be interpreted to encompass wider services and privileges, and many believe the treaties have not been honoured. Whether or not this is correct in some or many cases, the fact is the treaties affect only half the Indians of Canada. Most of the Indians of Quebec, British Columbia, and the Yukon are not parties to a treaty.

The terms and effects of the treaties between the Indian people and the Government are widely misunderstood. A plain reading of the words used in the treaties reveals the limited and minimal promises which were included in them. As a result of the treaties, some Indians were given an initial cash payment and were promised land reserved for their exclusive use, annuities, protection of hunting, fishing and trapping privileges subject (in most cases) to regulation, a school or teachers in most instances, and, in one treaty only, a medicine chest. There were some other minor considerations such as the annual provision of twine and ammunition.

The annuities have been paid regularly. The basic promise to set aside reserve land has been kept except in respect of the Indians of the Northwest Territories and a few bands in the northern parts of the Prairie Provinces. These Indians did not choose land when treaties were signed. The government wishes to see these obligations dealt with as soon as possible.

The right to hunt and fish for food is extended unevenly across the country and not always in relation to need. Although game and fish will become less and less important for survival as the pattern of Indian life continues to change, there are those who, at this time, still live in the traditional manner that their forefathers lived in when they entered into treaty with the government. The Government is prepared to allow such persons transitional freer hunting of migratory birds under the Migratory Birds Convention Act and Regulations.

The significance of the treaties in meeting the economic, educational, health and welfare needs of the Indian people has always been limited and will continue to decline. The services that have been provided go far beyond what could have been foreseen by those who signed the treaties.

The Government and the Indian people must reach a common understanding of the future role of the treaties. Some provisions will be found to have been discharged; others will have continuing importance. Many of the provisions and practices of another century may be considered irrelevant in the light of a rapidly changing society, and still others may be ended by mutual agreement. Finally, once Indian lands are securely within Indian control, the anomaly of treaties between groups within society and the government of that society will require that these treaties be reviewed to see how they can be equitably ended.

Other grievances have been asserted in more general terms. It is possible that some of these can be verified by appropriate research and may be susceptible of specific remedies. Others relate to aboriginal claims to land. These are so general and undefined that it is not realistic to think of them as specific claims capable of remedy except through a policy and program that will end injustice to Indians as members of the Canadian community. This is the policy that the government is proposing for discussion.

At the recent consultation meeting in Ottawa representatives of the Indians, chosen at each of the earlier regional meetings, expressed concern about the extent of their knowledge of Indian rights and treaties. They indicated a desire to undertake further research to establish their rights with greater precision, elected a National Committee on Indian Rights and Treaties for this purpose and sought government financial support for research.

The Government had intended to introduce legislation to establish an Indian claims Commission to hear and determine Indian claims. Consideration of the questions raised at the consultations and the review of Indian policy have raised serious doubts as to whether a Claims Commission as proposed to Parliament in 1965 is the right way to deal with the grievances of Indians put forward as claims.

The Government has concluded that further study and research are required by both the Indians and the Government. It will appoint a Commissioner who, in consultation with representatives of the Indians, will inquire into and report upon how claims arising in respect of the performance of the terms of treaties and agreements formally entered into by representatives of the Indians and the Crown, and the administration of moneys and lands pursuant to schemes established by legislation for the benefit of Indians may be adjudicated.

The Commissioner will also classify the claims that in his judgment ought to be referred to the courts or any special quasi-judicial body that may be recommended.

It is expected that the Commissioner's inquiry will go on concurrently with that of the National Indian Committee on Indian Rights and Treaties and the Commissioner will be authorized to recommend appropriate support to the Committee so that it may conduct research on the Indians' behalf and assist the Commissioner in his inquiry.

6 Indian Lands

Control of Indian lands should be transferred to the Indian people.

Frustration is as great a handicap as a sense of grievance. True cooperation and participation can come only when the Indian people are controlling the land which makes up the reserves.

The reserve system has provided the Indian people with lands that generally have been protected against alienation without their consent. Widely scattered across Canada, the reserves total nearly 6,000,000 acres and are divided into about 2,200 parcels of varying sizes. Under the existing system, title to reserve lands is held either by the Crown in the right of Canada or the Crown in right of one of the provinces. Administrative control and legislative authority are, however, vested exclusively in the government and the Parliament of Canada. It is a trust. As long as this trust exists, the Government, as a trustee, must supervise the business connected with the land.

The result of Crown ownership and the Indian Act has been to tie the Indian people to a land system that lacks flexibility and inhibits development. If an Indian band wishes to gain income by leasing its land, it has to do so through a cumbersome system involving the government as trustee. It cannot mortgage reserve land to finance development on its own initiative. Indian people do not have control of their lands except as the Government allows, and this is no longer acceptable to them. The Indians have made this clear at the consultation meetings. They now want real control, and this Government believes that they should have it. The Government recognizes that full and true equality calls for Indian control and ownership of reserve land.

Between the present system and the full holding of title in fee simple lie a number of intermediate states. The first step is to change the system under which ministerial decision is required for all that is done with Indian land. This is where the delays, the frustrations and the obstructions lie. The Indians must control their land.

This can be done in many ways. The Government believes that each band must make its own decision as to the way it wants to take control of its land and the manner in which it intends to manage it. It will take some years to complete the process of devolution.

The Government believes that full ownership implies many things. It carries with it the free choice of use, of retention or of disposition. In our society it also carries with it an obligation to pay for certain services. The government recognizes that it may not be acceptable to put all lands into the provincial systems immediately and make them subject to taxes. When the Indian people see that the only way that they can own and fully control land is to accept taxation the way other Canadians do, they will make that decision.

Alternative methods for the control of their lands will be made available to Indian individuals and bands. Whatever methods of land control are chosen by the Indian people, the present system under which the Government must execute all leases, supervise and control procedures and surrenders, and generally act as trustee, must be brought to an end. But the Indian land heritage should be protected. Land should be alienated from them only by the consent of the Indian people themselves. Under a proposed Indian Lands Act full management would be in the hands of the bands and, if the bands wish, they or individuals would be able to take title to their land without restrictions.

As long as the Crown controls the land for the benefit of bands who use and occupy it, it is responsible for determining who may, as a member of a band, share in the assets of band land. The qualifications for band membership which it has imposed are part of the legislation – the Indian Act – governing the administration of reserve lands. Under the present Act, the Government applies and interprets these qualifications. When bands take title to their lands, they will be able to define and apply these qualifications themselves.

The Government is prepared to transfer to the Indian people the reserve lands, full control over them and, subject to the proposed Indian Lands Act, the right to determine who shares in ownership. The Government proposes to seek agreements with the bands and, where necessary, with the governments of the provinces. Discussions will be initiated with the Indian people and the provinces to this end.

Implementation of the New Policy

1 Indian Associations and Consultation

Successful implementation of the new policy would require the further development of a close working relationship with the Indian community. This was made abundantly clear in the proposals set forth by the National Indian Brotherhood at the national meeting to consult on revising the Indian Act. Their brief succinctly identified the needs at that time and offers a basis for discussing the means of adaptation to the new policy.

To this end the government proposes to invite the executives of the National Indian Brotherhood and the various provincial associations to discuss the role they might play in the implementation of the new policy, and the financial resources they may require. The Government recognizes their need for independent advice, especially on legal matters. The government also recognizes that the discussions will place a heavy burden on Indian leaders during the adjustment period. Special arrangements will have to be made so that they may take the time needed to meet and discuss all aspects of the new policy and its implementation.

Needs and conditions vary greatly from province to province. Since the adjustments would be different in each case, the bulk of the negotiations would likely be with the provincial bodies, regional groups and the bands themselves. There are those matters which are of concern to all, and the National Brotherhood would be asked to act in liaison with the various provincial associations and with the federal departments which would have ongoing responsibilities.

The Government proposes to ask that the associations act as the principal agencies through which consultation and negotiations would be conducted, but each band would be consulted about gaining ownership of its land holdings. Bands would be asked to designate the association through which their broad interests would be represented.

2 Transitional Period

The Government hopes to have the bulk of the policy in effect within five years and believes that the necessary financial and other arrangements can be concluded so that Indians will have full access to provincial services within that time. It will seek an immediate start to the many discussions that will need to be held with the provinces and with representatives of the Indian people.

The role of the Department of Indian Affairs and Northern Development in serving the Indian people would be phased out as arrangements with the provinces were completed and remaining Federal Government responsibilities transferred to other departments.

The Commissioner will be appointed soon and instructed to get on with his work.

Steps would be taken in consultation with representatives of the Indian people to transfer control of land to them. Because of the need to consult over five hundred bands the process would take some time.

A policy can never provide the ultimate solutions to all problems. A policy can achieve no more than is desired by the people it is intended to serve. The essential feature of the Government's proposed new policy for Indians is that it acknowledges that truth by recognizing the central and essential role of the Indian people in solving their own problems. It will provide, for the first time, a non-discriminatory framework within which, in an atmosphere of freedom, the Indian people could, with other Canadians, work out their own destiny.

Notes

Introduction

1 *The Constitution Act, 1982*, s. 35(1).
2 The term 'Aboriginal peoples' is defined in section 35(2), which reads: 'In this Act, "Aboriginal peoples of Canada" includes the Indian, Inuit and Métis peoples of Canada.' There are problems with any collective term, but I prefer to use the term 'indigenous peoples' because it implies a more international understanding of the legal and political relationship, at least as it is understood by many indigenous peoples. I will use the term 'Aboriginal peoples' when I am specifically referring to the indigenous peoples of Canada.
3 To see the interesting evolution of Aboriginal rights law in Canada from pre–section 35(1) to the present, see Cumming and Mickenberg (1972); Slattery (1979); Rotman (1996); the Royal Commission on Aboriginal Peoples (1996); D. Russell (2000); McNeil (2001); and Borrows (2002).
4 There are a growing number of important cases; however, four of the main cases are *Calder v. Attorney-General of British Columbia*, [1973] S.C.R. 313; *R. v. Sparrow*, [1990] 1 S.C.R. 1075; *R. v. Van der Peet*, [1996] 2 S.C.R. 507; and *Delgamuukw v British Columbia*, [1997] 3 S.C.R.
5 George Erasmus, 'Introduction: Twenty Years of Disappointed Hopes,' in Richardson (1989), 1–2.
6 Department of Indian Affairs and Northern Development (1969).
7 Cairns (2000).
8 Kymlicka (1995).
9 There are a number of terms for those indigenous people who possess forms of knowledge rooted in indigenous nations – elders, wisdom keepers, medicine people. In this book I use the term 'indigenous philosophers'

for those indigenous people who are sources of indigenous ways of knowing the world and who are recognized by the people in their communities as possessing such knowledge. I should point out that there is not always agreement within communities about who these people are.

10 The Final Report was tabled in Parliament on 21 November 1996.

11 Alfred (1995, 1999); Borrows (2002).

12 I hope to show that the relationship between word warriors and indigenous philosophers is a complex one, but we must *begin* by situating word warriors as listeners and indigenous philosophers as teachers and guides. However, this relationship is not unidirectional. Indigenous philosophers need to appreciate the legitimacy and seriousness of the kinds of intellectual work word warriors do in mainstream society. I will discuss this separation of intellectual and political labour in chapter 5.

1 White Paper Liberalism and the Problem of Aboriginal Participation

1 Statement of the Government of Canada on Indian Policy (1969). The White Paper is reproduced in its entirety in appendix 1.

2 See Borrows (2002); Macklem (2001); Rotman (1996); McNeil (2001); D. Russell (2000); and Royal Commission (1996).

3 See Alfred (1999); Grand Council of the Crees of Quebec (1995); and Wa and Uukw (1992).

4 Three general sources that I have found useful are Kymlicka (1990); Gray (1995); and Rosenblum, (1989).

5 See Macklem (2001).

6 See McNeil (1998).

7 The total expenditures of the Indian Affairs Branch from 1964–5 to 1968–9 went from $64.8 million to $165.8 million. See Weaver (1981, 25). I have greatly benefited from this fine scholarship.

8 Cardinal (1969).

9 In terms of federal political parties, the Reform Party endorsed the White Paper as its position on Aboriginal rights in Canada. The provinces remain hostile to recognizing the Aboriginal right of self-government. See M.H. Smith (1990).

10 Flanagan (2000). Flanagan is now an Aboriginal policy adviser for the Conservative Party of Canada.

11 See Trudeau (1970, 1972).

12 Trudeau selected his Cabinet in June 1968 and appointed two Indian Affairs ministers: Jean Chrétien and Robert Andras. Eighteen meetings with Indian leaders were planned across Canada beginning in July 1968.

Indians were angered when the White Paper was released before these consultations could be incorporated into policy changes in DIAND. See S. Weaver (1981, 59–65).

13 For example, in the official response from the Indian Chiefs of Alberta, 'Citizens Plus,' the chiefs stated: 'We have studied carefully the contents of the White Paper on Indians and we have concluded that it offers despair instead of hope. Under the guise of land ownership, the government has devised a scheme whereby within a generation or shortly after the proposed Indian Lands Act expires our people would be left with no land and consequently the future generation would be condemned to the despair and ugly spectre of urban poverty in ghettos.' In Waubageshig (1970, 5).

14 From S. Weaver (1981, 52), Memo, Head of the Special Planning Secretariat to Gordon Robertson, 15 February 1967. For more exact figures see page 26.

15 See Indian Chiefs of Alberta (1970); Manitoba Indian Brotherhood (1971); Union of British Columbia Indian Chiefs (1970); and Association of Iroquois and Allied Indians (1971).

16 Graham and Abele (1996, 23).

17 *Guerin v. R.* rev'd (1984) 13 D.L.R. (4th) 321 (S.C.C.). For a detailed discussion of *Guerin* and the fiduciary relationship, see Rotman (1996), especially ch. 5). I am much indebted to this excellent study of the fiduciary relationship.

18 *St. Catherines Milling and Lumber Company Co. v. The Queen* (1888), 14 A.C. 46 (P.C.). For a more detailed and nuanced discussion of these four criteria see Cumming and Mickenberg (1972).

19 The relevant passage reads: 'We do, with the Advice of our Privy Council strictly enjoin and require, that no private Person do presume to make any Purchase from the said Indians of any Lands reserved to the said Indians, within those parts of our Colonies where, We have thought proper to allow Settlement; but that, if at any Time any of the said Indians should be inclined to dispose of the said Lands, the same shall be Purchased only for Us. In our name, at some Public meeting or Assembly of the said Indians, to be Held for the Purpose by the Governor or commander in Chief of our Colony respectively within which they shall lie' (R.S.C. 1970, Appendices, at pp. 127–9). Cited from Cumming and Mickenberg (1972, 291).

20 Rotman (1996, 70).

21 Rotman points out that 'whereas a fiduciary relationship is similar in nature to a trust relationship, the former does not depend on the existence of a property interest for its sustenance. Rather, its existence depends on the quality and character of the relationship between the parties which

gives rise to equitable obligations on the part of some, or all, of the parties in that relationship' (ibid., 4).

22 See Kulchyski (1994, 22).

23 See Cumming and Mickenberg (1972, n18). The original study undertaken by the Indian-Eskimo Association was written by legal scholar Douglas Sanders.

24 White Paper (reproduced in the appendix in this volume), emphasis added.

25 Ibid. 126. The phrase is repeated on page 130 of the appendix with the following sentence added: 'To argue against this right is to argue for discrimination, isolation and separation.'

26 Ibid., 127.

27 The idea that Indians constitute a 'burden on the Crown' comes from *St. Catherines Milling and Lumber Company Co. v. The Queen* (1888), 14 A.C. 46 (P.C.). For the ruling on the Nishga land claim, see *Calder v. A.G.B.C.* (1973), 34 D.L.R. (3d) 145, [1973] S.C.R. 313. For information regarding the 'Nisga'a' see their website, www.schoolnet.ca/aboriginal/nisga1/index-e.html. The right of self-determination is the right of a people to choose how they want to govern themselves. For a discussion of *Calder*, including the decision, see Kulchyski (1994, 61–126).

28 See Kulchyski (1994, 69).

29 Ibid., 117.

30 White Paper, 133 in appendix (emphasis added).

31 Ibid., 134.

32 For example, the second section of the Charter of Rights and Freedoms, titled Fundamental Rights, reads:

> Everyone has the following fundamental freedoms:
> *a*) freedom of conscience and religion;
> *b*) freedom of thought, belief, opinion and expression, including freedom of the press and other media of communication;
> *c*) freedom of peaceful assembly; and
> *d*) freedom of association.

33 Duncan Ivison (2003, 33) has a useful description of liberal governance: liberal governance presupposes that individuals are free, but free in the right way – free to exercise choice, to act rationally and reasonably, and to subject themselves to certain kinds of social and political obligations.

34 White Paper, 124, 126 in appendix.

35 Ibid., 139 in appendix.

36 See Williams (1990). See also Tully (1993, 137–76).

37 See Rawls (1971, 83; 1993, ch. 5).

38 It is interesting that the Royal Commission on Aboriginal Peoples recommended that Canadian governments enter into long-term economic development relationships with Aboriginal nations. See Recommendation 2.5.1. 'Federal, provincial and territorial governments enter into long-term economic development agreements with Aboriginal nations, or institutions representing several nations, to provide multi-year funding to support economic development.' In *Report of the Royal Commission on Aboriginal Peoples Report* (II. 1072).

39 Cardinal (1969, n8). For Trudeau's view of federalism, see his *Federalism and French Canadians* (1968).

40 Cardinal (1969, 1).

41 Ibid., 133.

42 Ibid., 166.

43 See Royal Commission on Aboriginal Peoples (1995).

44 In addition to Cardinal's book see Wabaghesig (1970); Manuel and Posluns (1974); Deloria (1969); Josephy (1971); and Forbes (1967). Not all indigenous writers defend indigenous nationhood; for an Indian writer who defends White Paper liberalism, see Wuttunee (1971).

45 See Deloria (2004, 16–30).

46 There is an enormous literature on the philosophical relationship between the individual and community and how we ought to think about political justice, but much of it does not address the sui generis nature of the Indigenous–European political relationship. Fortunately, there is a growing literature in contemporary political thought that considers indigenous rights as relevant to contemporary philosophical debates on political justice. For example, see Tully (1995); Ivison (2003); Kymlicka (1995c); M.S. Williams (1998); Laden (2001); Young (2000); Tomasi (2001); and Levy (2000).

47 This is similar to the American *Dawes Act* of 1887, known as the 'Allotment Act' in the United States. See Wilkins (2002); and Cornell (1989).

48 This unilateral action would effectively end the fiduciary responsibilities of the federal government. See Rotman (1996, 50–65).

49 The legal scholar Lee C. Buchheit defines colonialism as 'the domination of a people by foreign governors (with its attendant injury to national and cultural pride) and the inability of the colonial subjects to control their own political destiny, often coupled with a degree of economic exploitation and denial of human rights' (1978, 18). For an interesting contrast, the *Oxford English Dictionary* defines colonialism as 'the colonial system or principle. Now frequently used in the derogatory sense of an *alleged* policy of exploitation of backward or weak peoples by a large power' (emphasis added).

50 By 'our' I mean both Aboriginal and non-Aboriginal peoples' understandings of political justice.

51 The idea of fairness, measured among individuals, is one of the main ideas of John Rawls's liberal theory of justice. See Rawls (1971 and 1993, especially Lectures I and III).

52 See Flanagan (2000); Smith (1995); and Cairns (2000).

53 Some argue that they are not citizens of the Canadian state at all. See Alfred (1999).

54 McNeil (1998, 137).

55 Borrows (2002, 113).

56 Flanagan (2000, 4).

57 Engels in particular knew and admired the work of Lewis Henry Morgan in Iroquois Country. See Morgan (1993).

58 Flanagan's book won the Canadian Political Science Association's Donald Smiley Prize for 2001. The award is for best book in the study of government or politics. For a complete list of the propositions that he argues make up the Aboriginal orthodoxy see Flanagan (2000, 6–7).

59 Melvin Smith makes a statement that is similar in spirit to Flanagan's when he addresses the Royal Commission's claim that there are multiple sources for the aboriginal right of self-government: 'This is an astounding proposition. Even a first-year constitutional law student knows that the Constitution of Canada is the supreme law of the land and all other laws, customs, constitutions, treaties, and spiritual beliefs are subservient to it. There is no other basis on which to derive an inherent right to self-government than through the Canadian Constitution. The courts have told us over and over again that it is simply not here' (1995, 161–2).

60 Flanagan (2000, 31).

61 Ibid., 7.

2 Cairns's Canada: Citizens Nonplussed

1 See Cairns (1985, 1986, 1988, 1991, 1992, 1999). See also Bruner (1995).

2 Hawthorn (1966–7).

3 See Cairns (2000).

4 Indigenous or Aboriginal nationhood is how Aboriginal peoples themselves understand and articulate their political status in their relationship with the Canadian state. For example, see Alfred (2000).

5 Cairns (2000, 47).

6 Ibid., 91–7.

7 Ibid., 210.

8 Ibid., 90.

9 Ibid., 211 (emphasis added).

10 Some indigenous nations, such as the Haudenosaunee, do not consider themselves Canadians at all.

11 Cairns (2000, 92). *Citizens Plus*, p.92. I should mention that I am not Iroquoian and therefore no expert on Iroquoian political thought. I have benefited greatly from conversations with many Iroquoian people about the Great Law of Peace and the 'Two Row Wampum' (or Guswentha), and especially about the idea of the 'Good Mind.' The main purpose of the following discussion is to show that Iroquoian philosophy *is* deeply philosophical and complex and worthy of close study. I will argue in chapter 5 that *how* indigenous philosophy is brought out into mainstream intellectual culture, and *who* does so, matters for indigenous peoples. I am thankful to Vera Palmer (Tuscarora), Christopher Jocks (Mohawk), Audra Simpson (Mohawk), Charlie Patton (Mohawk), Taiaiake Alfred (Mohawk), Marlene Brant Castellano (Mohawk), and Michael Doxtator (Mohawk) for generously sharing Iroquoian philosophical thought with me.

12 Momaday (1969, 33 and 46).

13 This is not to imply that all European philosophy is done this way; indeed, I will show that there are a number of philosophers whose work can be of great use to indigenous intellectuals. I will discuss indigenous philosophy in greater detail in chapters 4 and 5.

14 The Iroquois Confederacy stretched across northern New York, encompassing five (later six) indigenous nations. From east to west, the nations were the Mohawk, Oneida, Onondaga, Cayuga, Seneca, and later the Tuscarora. I should point out that there is disagreement and controversy among Iroquoian people over the authenticity and interpretation of the Great Law of Peace, and especially over who has the cultural and political authority to speak for Iroquoian people.

15 See Tehanetorens (1993).

16 For example, see Tully (1995, 127–8).

17 Mitchell (1989, 109–10).

18 Think of this omission in this way: Would Cairns, a political theorist, criticize the work of John Rawls without mentioning his normative terms such as 'veil of ignorance,' 'burdens of judgment,' and 'overlapping consensus'?

19 The Great Law of Peace was brought to the Iroquois by a prophet known as the Peacemaker; see Parker (1991); Wallace (1997); and Dennis (1993).

20 See Brant (1997). His work was very influential for motivating me to think more carefully about the ethical dimensions of indigenous ways of being in the world.

21 This raises several difficult epistemological issues. For example, the notion

of scepticism in traditional indigenous thought functions in a different way than it is understood within the European philosophical tradition, at least since the time of Montaigne. To the extent of my limited knowledge of indigenous religious traditions, indigenous 'philosophers' do not question the existence of the Creator, it is a given. They do question how we ought to behave appropriately in the world. The principle of reciprocity functions in such a way that categorical imperatives are not imposed on people; rather, they are shown – usually by means of stories – and it is up to the listener to decide how to act on the story.

22 See Snow (1996).

23 The Condolence Ceremony is the central concept in Iroquoian philosophy. See Katlatont Gabriel-Doxtator and Kawanatatie (1995); and Thomas and Boyle (1994).

24 This has led to the expanding field of indigenous literary criticism. See Warrior (1995); Vizenor (1994); Cook-Lynn (1996); Momaday (1997); and Weaver (1997).

25 For example, Jake Thomas used to recite the Great Law at least once a year while publishing his ideas in *Teachings from the Longhouse.*

26 However, the oral traditions of indigenous peoples have not fared well in American and Canadian courts. See Wa and Uukw (1989). To see how this view was distorted by Canadian courts see Culhane (1998).

27 See 'Glossary of Figures of Speech in Iroquois Political Rhetoric,' in Jennings et al. (1985, 115).

28 If anything, referring to the Europeans as 'fathers' lessened the purported power relationship in the favour of the Iroquois. See Prucha (1984, esp. 5–29).

29 Tehanetorens (1993, 3) writes: 'Wampum strings served as credentials or as a certificate of authority. No Iroquois chief would listen to a messenger or pay attention to a report until he received official information through a runner who carried the proper wampum string or belt. Wampum guaranteed a message or a promise. Treaties meant nothing unless they were accompanied by wampum. Belts were given and received at treaties as seals of friendship.'

30 From Paper (1988, frontispiece, ch. 1).

31 Druke (1985, 85).

32 P.A. Wallace (1997, 40).

33 The concept of the 'good mind' is a difficult one in Iroquoian philosophy. Its similarity to European ideas of the Good and to questions around 'living the good life' are interesting and worthy of closer examination. I thank Vera Palmer and Christopher Jocks for their many hours of discussion on this fascinating dimension of Iroquoian philosophy.

34 Parker (1991, 10).

35 Grinde and Johanssen (1991, 29).

36 It is interesting to note the similarity of this view with the 'forced assimilation' view of the White Paper. This is one reason why I believe the Two
Row Wampum, as it is interpreted in the early colonial context, is insuffi-
cient for a contemporary political context and needs to be renewed in a
twenty-first-century context. Mohawk political thinker Taiaiake Alfred's
work should be viewed in this light. See Alfred (1995, 2000).

3 Liberalism's Last Stand: Minority Rights and the (Mis)recognition of Aboriginal Sovereignty

1 The two relevant sections I am referring to in the *Constitution Act, 1982* are
sections 15 and 35. Section 15(1) reads: 'Every individual is equal before
and under the law and has the right to the equal protection and equal
benefit of the law without discrimination based on race, national or ethnic
origin, colour, religion, sex, age or mental or physical disability.' However,
in section 15(2) a provision is made for affirmative action programs, which
can, in a sense, trump the rights laid out in section 15(1). Section 35 per-
tains specifically to Aboriginal peoples; section 35(1) reads: 'The existing
Aboriginal and treaty rights of the Aboriginal peoples of Canada are hereby recognized and affirmed.' The exact meaning and content of Aboriginal
rights that are 'hereby recognized and affirmed' remain controversial; this
has the consequence of confusing the relationship between the basic rights
of equality spelled out in section 15 and the Aboriginal rights protected by
section 35.

2 I am using the concept of indigenous, or Aboriginal, sovereignty in this
chapter to capture (albeit crudely) the special relationship that Aboriginal
peoples have to their territories. I could also couch this discussion in the
language of indigenous nationhood, but in this chapter I want to show
that the concept of sovereignty itself is problematic when we discuss Aboriginal rights. While I would argue that the special relationship Aboriginal peoples have to their territories also entails 'ownership' in the Western
legal tradition, I simply want Aboriginal sovereignty to be understood as
it is articulated in the languages and traditions of Aboriginal peoples
themselves. For example, the Gitxsan and Wet'suwet'en hereditary chiefs
characterize their sovereignty by stating that 'the ownership of territory is
a marriage of the Chief and the land. Each Chief has an ancestor who encountered and acknowledged the life of the land. From such encounters
come power. The land, the plants, the animals and the people all have
spirit – they all must be shown respect. That is the basis of our law.' See

Wa and Uukw (1992, 7). See also Treaty 7 Elders and Tribal Council (1996).

3 For accounts of Aboriginal conceptions of sovereignty or 'ownership' see Wa and Uukw (1992); Treaty 7 Elders and Tribal Council (1996); Grand Council of the Crees of Quebec (1995); and Wub-E-Ke-Niew (1995).

4 Kymlicka (1989b, 154). Hereafter cited as 'LCC.'

5 I will draw mainly from two sources: LCC and Kymlicka 1995c, hereafter cited as 'MC.' See also Kymlicka (1989a, 1990, 1991, 1992b, 1992c, 1993a, 1993b, 1995a, 1995b); and Kymlicka and Norman (1994).

6 LCC, 1.

7 Kymlicka draws mainly from Dworkin (1977 and 1985). See also Rawls (1971 and 1993).

8 For a few of the 'standard' communitarian critiques of liberalism see Alasdair MacIntyre (1981); Sandel (1982); Taylor (1990); and Walzer, (1983). For a good summary of the liberal–communitarian debate see Mulhall and Swift (1992). See also Mackinnon (1991) and Young (1990). For a discussion about 'thick' and 'thin' conceptions of culture see Geertz (1973, esp. ch. 1); and Clifford (1988, esp. ch. 12).

9 LCC, 12. See also MC, ch. 5.

10 LCC, 13; and MC, 81.

11 LCC, 13 (emphasis added).

12 Ibid.

13 MC, 76 (emphasis added).

14 Ibid., 76–7.

15 Ibid., 84.

16 See LCC, ch. 8. On page 166, Kymlicka says: 'Rawls's own argument for the importance of liberty as a primary good is also an argument for the importance of cultural membership as a good.'

17 MC, 10 (emphasis added).

18 Ibid., 11.

19 Strictly speaking, at least in the Canadian legal and political context, Aboriginal peoples were never 'conquered.' I take *conquered* to be the most destructive form of the 'overrun' practice of colonization. For example, the Beothuck of Newfoundland can be said to have been conquered, but only to the extent that they no longer exist. From an Aboriginal perspective, as long as an Aboriginal community is occupying a homeland it remains unconquered.

20 MC, 108.

21 This difference of philosophical opinion lies at the centre of contemporary debates in political liberalism. For views of the 'benign neglect' approach

see Glazer (1975 and 1983). In the Aboriginal context see M.H. Smith (1995). For example, Smith states: 'A new native policy must be built on the twin principles of jurisdictional integration for natives within the mainstream of Canadian society, thus enhancing a sense of self reliance and personal achievement, and on the principle of equality under the law consistent with the rule of law and the Constitution. Moreover, such a policy must be formulated and implemented absent any sense of collective guilt over what may have happened in times past. Until now, this sense of guilt has been allowed to hang like a pall over all effects at native policy reform' (1995, 264).

22 Kymlicka includes the English and the French as holding prior occupancy because they were self-governing entities at the time the Canadian state was formed; however, Aboriginal peoples think of prior occupancy in the context of the time *before* the arrival of the Europeans. The difference between the two interpretations is that in Kymlicka's view we don't question the legitimacy of French and English sovereignty before the time of Confederation.

23 The distinction between Aboriginal peoples and immigrants is important for Kymlicka because it lays out the differences in political powers each holds within the Canadian state; in Kymlicka's theory, immigrant groups are not entitled to rights of self-governance.

24 MC, 110.

25 See Dickason (1995); and especially volume I of *Report of the Royal Commission on Aboriginal Peoples* (1996).

26 For example, see Hildebrandt et al. (1996); and Monet and Skanu'u (1992). Cf. note 3.

27 See Wa and Uukw, note 2.

28 For the purposes of my argument, I assume that there is a legitimate Aboriginal political entity that can negotiate with the provincial and federal governments. I am aware that I have simplified the process whereby a 'legitimate' voice arises from within an indigenous community; however, for the most part, indigenous peoples can and do have legitimate forms of political representation.

29 For example, Aboriginal leaders are used as 'consultants' at First Ministers' Conferences; that is, they do not speak for themselves about the content of their 'special' rights, just as they are excluded from most discussions about Aboriginal policy unless they engage the existing discourses of section 35(1) and the *Indian Act*.

30 In particular, see Tully (1995) and the Royal Commission's final report (1996), especially volume I.

31 This is why the Royal Commission began its final report with an examination of the historical relationship. I also believe, from my experience
working at the Royal Commission, that one of the main reasons for the
delay in submitting the final report was that the commissioners needed
time to work through some of the consequences of asserting that contemporary views of Aboriginal sovereignty have been distorted by particular
interpretations of history. The commission wanted to include Aboriginal
interpretations of history, but had to do so in a largely non-Aboriginal
intellectual and political environment – an environment which assumes
that Aboriginal interpretations do not count as legitimate.

32 MC, 116.

33 Ibid.

34 I mean this in the way Western political theorists construe the meaning of
'citizen.' For example, *Black's Law Dictionary* defines citizens as 'members
of community inspired to a common goal, who, in associated relations,
submit themselves to rules of conduct for the promotion of general welfare and conservation of individual as well as collective rights.'

35 I say that Aboriginal peoples *may* have relinquished their sovereignty
because Kymlicka leaves it as an open issue whether the possibility exists
that some communities remain sovereign – for example, the Cree of
northern Quebec, the Mohawk of Kahnawake, and the Gitxsan and
Wet'suwet'en people of British Columbia.

36 Waldron's argument basically states that although the lands taken from
Aboriginal peoples may have been unjustly taken at some time in the
distant past, it does not follow that Aboriginal peoples have just claims to
these lands at the present time. He argues that the rights of Aboriginal
peoples, and their moral claims of ownership to their lands, may have
been superseded by time itself. Now that many generations of European
settlers have settled on Aboriginal lands, it is the Europeans who have
legitimate moral claims of ownership, and who are, in a sense, innocent
victims in the recent surge in Aboriginal land claims. Waldron's view
ignores the significance of the political relationship between Aboriginal
peoples and the European newcomers; his argument amounts to a philosophical sleight of hand designed not just to condone the stealing of
Aboriginal lands but to absolve contemporary governments of responsibility for taking action to resolve outstanding Aboriginal land claims. See
Waldron (1997 and 2003). See also Thompson (2002).

37 Of course, this is not to say that compensation ought not play a role in
renewing the relationship.

38 I say 'some' because there were (and are) Europeans who embraced

Aboriginal ways of thinking. However, some of the better-known European philosophers – for example, Las Casas, Hobbes, Locke, Rousseau, and Tocqueville, whose works are considered to be essential to the Western canon – held colonial views of indigenous peoples.

4 Word Warriors

1 This remark begins the Royal Commission on Aboriginal Peoples' final report. Jim Bourque was an important Métis leader whose influence on the commission was profound, albeit brief. Sadly, Jim passed away before the final report was released, which makes the spirit of his words all the more important for those he left behind.

2 I am using the concepts of rights, sovereignty, and nationhood in this chapter to capture the legal and political significance of the sui generis relationship that Aboriginal peoples have to their territories. The explanations of rights, sovereignty, and nationhood I am most concerned with are ones articulated by Aboriginal peoples themselves. For example, the Eeyouch of Eeyou Astchee (Cree of Northern Quebec) state that for 'countless generations we have carefully looked after the land and all the creatures that inhabit it. Central to our values has always been the idea of sharing. As an elderly Cree told his nephew when handing down to him custody of the family land, 'You will look after this land, take care of it as a white man would his garden. It is up to you to protect, preserve, make rules where necessary and enforce good hunting practices. You will look after it as I have shown you in the past. You will also look after your people and share what you have on the land.' See Grand Council of the Crees (1998, 17). See also chapter 3, note 2.

3 See Rotman (1996).

4 I want to make it clear from the beginning that I am concerned with only one dimension of the Aboriginal – Canadian state relationship; that is, the legal and political practices that largely determine the content of Aboriginal rights discourse in Canada. I am thinking of Supreme Court Justices, judges, policy makers and analysts, professors, and Aboriginal leaders.

5 As I stated in the introduction, 'indigenous philosophers' are indigenous people who are recognized in their communities as the authentic sources of indigenous knowledge. I realize that it is not always easy for a community to agree who these people are; my point is that these people do exist (which is controversial enough for many White Paper liberals) and that they play a normative role in explaining indigenous ways of knowing the world.

6 See Borrows (2002, 140).

7 See Office of the Prime Minister Brian Mulroney (1991).

8 Tully (1995 and 2002).

9 See Wittgenstein (2001); Skinner (2003); and Foucault (2000).

10 A word about what I mean by 'serious.' A legal and political issue is 'serious' when the survival of the community is at stake, and most indigenous legal and political issues have some indigenous right, or rights, at stake. Word warriors incorporate the gravity of this political context into their work; in other words, they engage legal and political issues with the attitude that the well-being of indigenous communities is always at stake.

11 This statement demands a brief comment on what I mean by 'survival.' By way of an example, consider the philosophy of John Locke. One can engage Locke as a political philosopher, as an epistemologist, or to a lesser extent as a metaphysician. That is, Locke can be studied as a central figure in the European philosophical tradition. Aboriginal intellectuals should study Locke in this context, too, but should also read him as an esteemed thinker whose theory of property and views on political sovereignty were explicitly *used* to justify the dispossession of indigenous lands in the New World. This second kind of investigation, constitutive of what I will call in the next chapter 'critical indigenous philosophy,' is important because it helps explain why indigenous understandings of who they are as political nations have been marginalized from the earliest times. Of course, it is another issue whether these kinds of investigations yield results in, say, the form of favourable land claim negotiations and Supreme Court decisions. Since the outcomes of these legal and political practices have potentially brutal consequences to the well-being of Aboriginal communities, I'm suggesting that we must pay closer attention to the way we assemble our reminders, and how we use them in these more explicitly political contexts. See Turner (2004a).

12 See Borrows (2002); and McNeil (1998 and 2001).

13 Kymlicka (1989b, 154). For the complete quote, see page xx.

14 Just as it is impossible for many liberals to think about the ontological possibility of attaching rights to groups, for indigenous peoples it does not make sense to think that they possess the right to give away all of their territories. This is because most indigenous peoples think of themselves – ontologically – as inextricably woven into their homelands.

15 The final report was tabled in Parliament on 21 November 1996.

16 For the official mandate see *The Mandate: Royal Commission on Aboriginal Peoples*, federal Order in Council dated 26 August 1991, reference P.C. 1991–1597.

17 The final report consists of five volumes and is over 3,200 pages long.

18 For a copy of the final report in its entirety see www.ainc-inac.gc.ca/ch/
rcap/index_e.html. In his address for the launch of the final report,
George Erasmus stated: 'We criss-crossed the country, often working in
three separate teams. By the end of 1993, we had visited 96 communities,
held 178 days of hearings, heard briefs from 2067 people and accumulated
more than 76,000 pages of testimony.'

19 Of the four Aboriginal commissioners – George Erasmus, Paul Chartrand,
Viola Robinson, and Mary Sillett – only Chartrand had a legal background. He had published a book on Métis land rights, and he continues
to consult on Aboriginal affairs in Canada. Of the three non-Aboriginal
commissioners, Bertha Wilson was a former Supreme Court judge, Peter
Meekison was a professor of political science and former Deputy Minister
of Intergovernmental Affairs in Alberta, and René Dussault was a Quebec
Superior Court judge.

20 RCAP, 1996, vol. II, part 2, recommendation 2.3.2, page 1032, states that 'all
governments in Canada recognize that Aboriginal peoples are nations
vested with the right of self-determination.'

21 RCAP 1996, vol. I, 678.

22 Ibid.

23 Ibid., 682.

24 Ibid., 685.

25 Ibid., 689.

26 Ibid., 688.

27 There is no shortage of examples of the wholesale theft and destruction of
indigenous 'natural resources': forests in British Columbia, oil in Alberta,
fish in Nova Scotia and New Brunswick, and hydroelectric projects in
Ontario and especially Quebec.

28 The situation is bleaker when we examine White Paper liberalism, because
the imperative for change does not arise at all within its view of justice –
in fact, for White Paper liberals, justice demands that Aboriginal peoples
change *their* attitudes about equality, history, and justice.

29 The beginning of the 'Terms of Reference' for RCAP's mandate reads: 'The
Commission of Inquiry should investigate the evolution of the relationship among aboriginal peoples (Indian, Inuit, and Métis), the Canadian
government, and Canadian society as a whole. It should propose specific
solutions, rooted in domestic and international experience, to the problems which have plagued those relationships and which confront aboriginal peoples today.' Federal Order in Council dated 26 August 1991,
reference P.C. 1991–1597.

30 RCAP (1996, vol. II) recommendation 2.3.2, page 180.
31 Ibid., part 1, page 172. Emphasis added. Some Aboriginal peoples would claim that 'grave oppression' already defines the contemporary relationship.
32 The commission's mandate was problematic for indigenous nationalists right from its inception. Indigenous nationalists defend the position that Aboriginal peoples still own their lands in the richest sense of ownership, and that the legitimacy of this form of ownership lies *outside* the jurisdiction – and therefore the legitimacy – of the Canadian state. Indigenous nationalists emphasize the political powers their nations have retained throughout the history of the political relationship, as opposed to what powers have been lost through the unilateral assertion of Canadian sovereignty.
33 See RCAP (1996, vol. II), 213–23.
34 For example, recommendation 2.3.4 on the inherent right of self-government states in (d): 'The inherent right of self-government has a substantial degree of immunity from federal and provincial legislative acts, *except where*, in the case of federal legislation, it can be justified under a strict constitutional standard' (emphasis added).
35 For example, Aboriginal rights exist, but they are limited in how they may be exercised.
36 One just has to look at the contemporary political landscape: the Haida logging dispute in British Columbia, Mi'kmaq fishing rights in New Brunswick, and the Haudenosaunee's ongoing tax disputes with American and Canadian governments.
37 See Turner (2004b).
38 *Delgamuukw v British Columbia* [1997] 3 S.C.R. The case is published in its entirety, with commentary, in Stan Persky (1998). For additional commentaries see Borrows (1999); and Christie (2000). For background on the case see Cassidy (1992); Culhane (1998); and Mills (1992).
39 Persky (1998, 41).
40 Ibid., 32.
41 *R v. Van der Peet* [1996] 2 S.C.R. 507. For critiques of the case see Borrows (1997b); and Barsh and Henderson (1997).
42 Borrows (1997b, 37).
43 See *Van der Peet*, 508 (emphasis added).
44 Ibid., 510.
45 Tully (1995, 1).
46 Ibid., 17–18.
47 Ibid., 74 and 122.

48 Ibid., 211.

49 Ibid., 212.

50 Saul Bellow is reported to have said that when the Zulus produce a Tolstoy we'll read him. Indigenous peoples can counter by saying that when the White man produces a Peacemaker, we'll listen to him.

51 See Tully (2002).

52 Ibid., 537–8.

53 RCAP (1993).

54 See Johnston (1976); Wu-be-ken-iew (1995); (1968); and Vecsey (1983).

55 For example, the idea that individual rights can serve as a practical means of protecting oneself against the unjust intrusions of others is a decidedly modern European concept.

56 It is always easier to make this point by examining European philosophers from the past. For example, the early social contract theorists (Hobbes, Locke, and Rousseau) explained the social contract by distinguishing between the state of nature and a civil society. Indigenous peoples were definitively placed in the state of nature, to be used as barbaric objects of comparison for the highly evolved European civil society. Unpacking the significance of these philosophical claims and their relationship to colonialism is one responsibility of an indigenous intellectual culture.

57 Warrior (1995, 97–8).

58 Ibid., 123.

59 Ibid., 124.

60 See Slattery (1983, 1992); Clark (1990); Macklem (1993); and McNeil (1982).

61 See Borrows (1985, 1992a, 1992b, 1994, 1996, 1997b, 1997c). See also Henderson and Barsh (1982); D.M Johnston (1989); and Turpel (1993, p. 174).

62 Trigger and Washburn (1996, vol. I, xvii).

63 Alfred (1999, 97).

64 I will say more about this relationship in the next chapter.

65 See Said (1994, 64 and 100).

5 Towards a Critical Indigenous Philosophy

1 When the term 'philosophy' is italicized I mean it to be understood in a kind of cross-cultural context – that is, as a dialogical process between indigenous philosophy and European philosophy. I will say more about this process in this chapter and raise some of the difficulties with thinking about philosophical discourse in this way.

2 In 2003, the American Indians in Philosophy Association (AIPA) reported

that there were fewer than five American Indians employed in American university philosophy departments.

3 Three classics in the field of African colonialism are Cesaire (2000), Fanon (1967), *The Wretched of the Earth*; and Albert Memmi (1967), *The Colonizer and the Colonized*.

4 Appiah (1992).

5 Ibid., 92.

6 Ibid., 93.

7 Ibid., 94.

8 Or American Indian philosophy, Native philosophy, Anishnabi philosophy, Navajo philosophy, and so on.

9 For a publication on the Midewewin, see Johnston (1976); and Wub-E-Ke-Niew (1995).

10 Neihardt (1932).

11 See Clifford Geertz, 'Thick Description: Toward an Interpretive Theory of Culture,' in *The Interpretation of Cultures* (New York: Basic Books, 1973).

12 It is interesting to think about the other side of the relationship: indigenous philosophy done by a European philosopher.

13 For a fascinating book about the relationship between Heidegger and colonialism see McCumber (1999).

14 In this I am in complete agreement with the work of Deloria, Cook-Lynn, and more recently Alfred. See Cook-Lynn (1997).

15 Fixico (2003).

16 This is to set aside the more obvious objection about attributing a common metaphysics to all American Indians.

17 See Quine (1980).

18 Fixico's book is interesting for another reason. Fixico is an academic – indeed, a full professor – so he knows that once his work is published it is open to criticism; but many interested American Indians will most certainly receive his book differently. The idea of 'criticism' is itself a problematic concept, and therefore up for negotiation in a *philosophical* dialogue, and it ought to play a more central role in the cross-cultural dialogue between the various ways of thinking about the world.

19 Williams (1992).

20 Williams (1997, 3).

21 See Mihesuah (1998); and Mihesuah and Wilson (2004).

22 See Deloria (1998); Forbes (1988); and Medicine (2001).

23 Cook-Lynn (1997).

24 Cook-Lynn states in another essay (1999, 17): 'One of the traits that distinguishes native American Studies as an academic discipline (a trait much

maligned but finding its origins in those early times) is its demand that its intelligentsia expose the lies of the self-serving colonial academic institutions of America, bolster the right and obligation to disobedience, and resist the tyranny of the U.S. fantasies concerning history and justice and morality.'

25 Ibid., 27.

26 Ibid.

27 The term 'methodologies' is controversial in the social sciences; using a methodology raises, among other things, epistemological issues. Indigenous intellectuals have their own methodologies, and part of their responsibilities as word warriors is to defend the legitimacy of their methods as cogently as possible. See L.T. Smith (1999).

28 Yet Cook-Lynn is no anti-intellectual; she has written brilliant critiques of European ideas. See Cook-Lynn (1996).

29 As interpreted by the Great Law of Peace.

30 Alfred (1999, xiii), emphasis added.

31 Ibid., 2–3.

32 Deloria's writings are extensive. See 1988, 1992.

33 Alfred (1999, 23).

34 Ibid., 70–1.

35 Ibid., 70.

36 Of course, intellectual culture involves much more than developing legal and political strategies to be put to use in the political relationship with the state. My claim is that an indigenous intellectual culture can only thrive from within a secure political relationship with the state.

37 For recent work on indigenous legal and political thought see Christie (2000); Simpson (2003); Wilkins (2002); Jeff Corntassle (forthcoming); and Wilkinson (2005).

38 Monture-Angus (1999, 9).

39 Ibid., 160.

40 Alfred does not want to have this discussion in the language of rights, but providing reasons why the discourse of rights does not work for indigenous peoples is itself part of the dialogical process between word warriors and mainstream intellectual culture.

41 I say 'as best we can' because I believe we cannot know for sure what, say, Locke meant by 'property' or Hobbes meant by 'sovereignty'; this is why we have ongoing dialogues about interpreting the history of ideas. I say 'on its own terms' because we can only understand the meaning of a term by seeing how it was used in a particular context; once again, this involves interpretation, which is why we have ongoing dialogues about interpret-

ing the history of ideas. Both these statements are grounded in the Wittgensteinian claim that ongoing interpretation does not guarantee consensus; rather, it guarantees that no matter what one says, it is always open to disagreement.

42 Wittgenstein (1990, 189).
43 Garroutte (2003, 10 and 113). I should point out that her use of the term 'seriously' in 'can take philosophies of knowledge carried by indigenous peoples seriously' is never explained. See chapter 4, note 10.
44 Kymlicka (1989, 154).

Bibliography

Alfred, Taiaiake. 1995. *Heeding the Voices of Our Ancestors: Kahnawake Mohawk Politics and the Rise of Native Nationalism in Canada*. Oxford: Oxford University Press.
– 1999. *Peace, Power, and Righteousness*. Oxford: Oxford University Press.
Appiah, Kwame Anthony. 1992. *In My Father's House: Africa in the Philosophy of Culture*. New York: Oxford University Press.
Association of Iroquois and Allied Indians. 1971. *Position Paper*. Brantford, ON.
Barsh, Russel Lawrence, and James (sakej) Henderson. 1997. 'The Supreme Court's Van der Peet Trilogy: Native Imperialism and Ropes of Sand.' *McGill Law Journal* 42:993.
Borrows, John. 1984. 'Constitutional Law from a First Nation Perspective: Self-Government and the Royal Proclamation.' *University of British Columbia Law Review* 28:1.
– 1985. 'Contemporary Traditional Equality: The Effect of the Charter on First Nations Politics.' In David Schneiderman and Kate Sutherland, eds., *Charting the Consequences: The Impact of Charter Rights on Canadian Law and Politics*. Toronto: University of Toronto Press.
– 1992a. 'A Genealogy of Law: Inherent Sovereignty and First Nations Self-Government.' *Osgoode Hall Law Journal* 30:291.
– 1992b. 'Negotiating Treaties and Land Claims: The Impact of Diversity within First Nations Property Interests.' *Wind Y.B. Access Justice* 12:179.
– 1996. 'With or Without You: First Nations Law in Canada.' *McGill Law Journal* 41:629.
– 1997a. 'Frozen Rights in Canada: Constitutional Interpretation and the Trickster.' *American Indian Law Review* 11:37.
– 1997b. 'The Trickster: Integral to a Distinctive Culture.' *Constitutional Forum* 8(2).

- 1999. 'Sovereignty's Alchemy: An Analysis of *Delgamuukw v. The Queen.'*
  Osgoode Hall Law Journal 37:537.
- 2002. *Recovering Canada: The Resurgence of Indigenous Law.* Toronto: University of Toronto Press.
Brant, Clare M.D. 1997. 'A Collection of Chapters, Lectures, Workshops and
  Thoughts.' Private manuscript.
Bruner, Edward, ed. 1995. *Reconfigurations: Canadian Citizenship and Constitutional Change.* Toronto: McClelland & Stewart.
Buchheit, Lee C. 1978. *Seccession, the Legitimacy of Self-Determination.* New
  Haven, CT: Yale University Press.
Cairns, Allan C. 1985. *Constitutionalism, Government, and Society in Canada.*
  Toronto: University of Toronto Press.
- 1986. *The Politics of Gender, Ethnicity, and Language in Canada.* Toronto:
  University of Toronto Press.
- 1988. *Constitution, Government, and Society in Canada.* Toronto: McClelland &
  Stewart.
- 1991. *Disruptions: Constitutional Struggles, from the Charter to Meech Lake.*
  Toronto: McClelland & Stewart.
- 1999. *Citizenship, Diversity, and Pluralism: Canadian and Comparative Perspectives.* Montreal: McGill–Queen's University Press.
- 2000. *Citizens Plus: Aboriginal Peoples and the Canadian State.* Vancouver: UBC
  Press.
- 2002. *Charter versus Federalism: The Dilemmas of Constitutional Reform.*
  Montreal: McGill-Queen's University Press.
Cardinal, Harold. 1969. *The Unjust Society: The Tragedy of Canada's Indians.*
  Edmonton, AB: Hurtig.
Cassidy, Frank, ed. 1992. *Delgamuukw v. the Queen: Aboriginal Title in British
  Columbia.* Montreal: Institute for Research on Public Policy.
Cesaire, Aimee. 2000. *Discourse on Colonialism,* trans. Joan Pinkham. New
  York: Monthly Review Press.
Christie, Gordon. 2000. '*Delgamuukw* and the Protection of Aboriginal Land
  Interests.' *University of Ottawa Law Review* 32:85.
Clarke, Bruce. 1990. *Native Liberty, Crown Sovereignty: The Existing Aboriginal
  Right of Self-Government in Canada.* Montreal: McGill-Queen's University
  Press.
Clifford, James. 1988. *The Predicament of Culture: Twentieth-Century Ethnography, Literature, and Art.* Cambridge, MA: Harvard University Press.
Cook-Lynn, Elizabeth. 1996. *Why I Can't Read Wallace Stegner and Other Essays:
  A Tribal Voice.* Madison: University of Wisconsin Press.
- 1997. 'Who Stole Native American Studies?' *Wacazo Sa Review* (Fall).

– 1999. 'American Indian Studies: An Overview.' *Wacazo Sa Review* (Fall).

Cornell, Stephen. 1989. *The Return of the Native*. Oxford: Oxford University Press.

Corntassle, Jeff. (forthcoming). *Forced Federalism: Contemporary Indian Challenges to American Indian Sovereignty*. Norman: University of Oklahoma Press.

Culhane, Dara. 1998. *At the Pleasure of the Crown: Anthropology, Law and First Nations*. Burnaby: Talonbooks.

Cumming, Peter A., and Neil H. Micklenberg, eds. 1972. *Native Rights in Canada*. Toronto: General Publishing.

Deloria, Vine. 1969. *Custer Died for Your Sins: An Indian Manifesto*. London: Collier-Macmillan.

– 1988. *Custer Died for Your Sins: An Indian Manifesto*. Norman: University of Oklahoma Press.

– 1992. *God Is Red: A Native View of Religion*. Golden, CO: North American Press.

– 2004. 'Marginal and Submarginal.' In Devon Abbott Mihesuah and Angela Cavender Wilson, eds., *Indigenizing the Academy: Transforming Scholarship and Empowering Communities*. Lincoln: University of Nebraska Press.

Dennis, Matthew. 1993. *Cultivating a Landscape of Peace: Iroquois-European Encounters in Seventeenth-Century America*. Ithaca, NY: Cornell University Press.

Department of Indian Affairs and Northern Development. 1969. *Statement of the Government of Canada on Indian Policy 1969*. Ottawa: Queen's Printer.

Dickason, Olive Patricia, ed. 1995. *The Native Imprint: The Contribution of First Peoples to Canada's Character*. Vol. 1, *To 1815*. Edmonton: Athabaska University Press.

Druke, Mary A. 1977. *Taking Rights Seriously*. London: Duckworth.

– 1985. 'Iroquois Treaties: Common Forms, Varying Interpretations, in Iroquois Diplomacy.' In Jennings et al., eds., *The History and Culture of Iroquois Diplomacy*. Syracuse, NY: Syracuse University Press.

Fanon, Franz. 1967. *The Wretched of the Earth*. Trans. Constance Farrington. New York: Grove Press.

Fixico, Donald. 2003. *The American Indian Mind in a Linear World: American Indian Studies and Traditional Knowledge*. New York: Routledge.

Flanagan, Thomas. 2000. *First Nations? Second Thoughts*. Montreal: McGill-Queen's University Press.

Forbes, Jack D. 1967. *Nevada Indians Speak*. Reno: University of Nevada Press.

– 1988. *Black Africans and Native Americans: Color, Evolution, and Caste in the Evolution of Red-Black Peoples*. New York: Blackwell.

Foucault, Michel. 2000. *Power: Essential Works of Foucault 1954–1984*. Ed. James D. Faubion. Trans. Robert Hurley et al. New York: The New Press.

Garroutte, Eva-Marie. 2003. *Real Indians: Identity and the Survival of Native America*. Berkeley: University of California Press.

Geertz, Clifford. 1973. 'Thick Description: Toward an Interpretive Theory of Culture.' In *The Interpretation of Cultures*. New York: Basic Books.

Glazer, Nathan. 1975. *Affirmative Discrimination: Ethnic Inequality and Public Policy*. New York: Basic Books.

– 1983. *Ethical Dilemmas: 1964–1982*. Cambridge, MA: Harvard University Press.

Graham, Katherine, and Frances Abele. 1996. *Public Policy and Aboriginal Peoples, 1965–1992*. 2 vols. Ottawa: Canada Communication Group.

Grand Council of the Crees. 1998. *Never without Consent: Stand against Forcible Inclusion into an Independent Quebec*. Toronto: ECW Press.

Grand Council of the Crees of Quebec [Eeyou Astchee]. 1995. *Sovereign Injustice: Forcible Inclusion of the James Bay Cree and Cree Territory into a Sovereign Quebec*. Nemaska, PQ: Eeyou Astchee, Grand Council of the Crees.

Gray, John. 1995. *Liberalism*. Minneapolis: University of Minnesota Press.

Grinde, Donald, and Bruce Johanssen. 1991. *Exemplar of Liberty: Native America and the Evolution of Democracy*. Los Angeles: American Indian Studies Center, University of California, Los Angeles.

Hawthorn, E.B. 1966–7. *A Survey of the Contemporary Indians of Canada*, 2 vols. Ottawa: Queen's Printer.

Henderson, James (sakej) Youngblood, and Russell Barsh. 1982. 'Aboriginal Rights, Treaty Rights, and Human Rights: Tribes and Constitutional Renewal.' *Journal of Canadian Studies* 17:55.

Hildebrandt, Walter, Dorothy First Rider, and Sarah Carter. 1996. *Treaty 7 Elders and Tribal Council: The True Spirit and Original Intent of Treaty 7*. Montreal: McGill–Queen's University Press.

Indian Chiefs of Alberta. *Citizens Plus*. Edmonton, AB.

Ivison, Duncan. 2003. *Postcolonial Liberalism*. Cambridge: Cambridge University Press.

Jennings, Francis, et al., eds. 1985. *The History and Culture of Iroquois Diplomacy*. Syracuse, NY: Syracuse University Press.

Johnston, Basil. 1976. *Ojibway Heritage*. Toronto: McClelland & Stewart.

Johnston, Darlene M. 1989. *The Taking of Indian Lands in Canada: Consent or Coercion*. Saskatoon: University of Saskatchewan Native Law Centre.

Josephy, Alvin M. 1971. *Red Power*. New York: American Heritage Press.

Katlatont Gabriel-Doxtator, Brenda, and Arlette Kawanatatie. 1995. *At the Woods' Edge: An Anthology of the History of the People of Kanesata:ke*. Kanesata:ke, PQ: Kanesatake Education Center.

Kulchyski, Peter, ed. 1994. *Unjust Relations: Aboriginal Rights in Canadian Courts.* Toronto: Oxford University Press.

Kymlicka, Will. 1989a. 'Liberal Individualism and Liberal Neutrality.' *Ethics* 99(4):883–905.

– 1989b. *Liberalism, Community, and Culture.* Oxford: Oxford University Press.

– 1990. *Contemporary Political Philosophy: An Introduction.* Oxford: Oxford University Press.

– 1991. 'Liberalism and the Politicization of Ethnicity.' *Canadian Journal of Law and Jurisprudence* 4(2):239–56.

– 1992a. *Recent Work in Citizenship Theory.* Ottawa: Multiculturalism and Citizenship Canada.

– 1992b. 'The Rights of Minority Cultures: Reply to Kukathas.' *Political Theory* 20(1):140–6.

– 1992c. 'Two Models of Pluralism and Tolerance.' *Analyse und Kritik* 14(1): 33–56.

– 1993a. 'Group Representation in Canadian Politics.' In L. Seidle, ed., *Equity and Community: The Charter, Interest Advocacy, and Representation.* Montreal: Institute for Research on Public Policy.

– 1993b. 'Reply to Modood.' *Analyse und Kritik* 15(1):92–6.

– 1995. *Multicultural Citizenship: A Liberal Theory of Minority Rights.* Oxford: Oxford University Press.

Kymlicka, Will, and W.J. Norman. 2001. 'Return of the Citizen.' *Ethics* 104(2):352–81.

Laden, Anthony Simon. 2001. *Reasonably Radical: Deliberative Liberalism and the Politics of Identity.* Ithaca, NY: Cornell University Press.

Landes, Ruth. 1968. *Ojibwa Religion and the Midewiwin.* Madison: University of Wisconsin Press.

Levy, Jacob. 2000. *The Multiculturalism of Fear.* Oxford: Oxford University Press.

MacIntyre, Alasdair. 1981. *After Virtue.* London: Duckworth.

Mackinnon, Catharine. 1991. *Toward a Feminist Theory of the State.* Cambridge, MA: Harvard University Press.

Macklem, Patrick. 1993. 'Distributing Sovereignty: Indian Nations and the Equality of Peoples.' *Stanford Law Review* 45(5):1312–67.

– 2001. *Indigenous Difference and the Constitution of Canada.* Toronto: University of Toronto Press.

Manitoba Indian Brotherhood. 1971. *Wahbung: Our Tomorrows.* Winnipeg, MB: MIB.

Manuel, George, and George Posluns. 1974. *The Fourth World: An Indian Reality.* Don Mills, ON: Collier-Macmillan Canada.

McCumber, John. 1999. *Metaphysics and Oppression: Heidegger's Challenge to Western Philosophy*. Bloomington: Indiana University Press.

McNeil, Kent. 1982. 'The Constitutional Rights of the Aboriginal Peoples of Canada.' *Supreme Court Law Review* 4:255.

– 1998. 'The Meaning of Aboriginal Title.' In Michael Asch, ed., *Aboriginal and Treaty Rights in Canada: Essays on Law, Equality, and Respect for Difference.* Vancouver: UBC Press.

– 2001. *Emerging Justice: Essays on Indigenous Rights in Canada and Australia.* Saskatoon: Native Law Centre, University of Saskatchewan.

Medicine, Beatrice. 2001. *Learning to Be an Anthropologist and Remaining 'Native': Selected Writings.* Ed. Sue-Ellen Jacobs. Urbana: University of Illinois Press.

Memmi, Albert. 1967. *The Colonizer and the Colonized.* Boston: Beacon Press.

Mihesuah, Devon, ed. 1998. *Natives and Academics: Researching and Writing sbout American Indians.* Lincoln: University of Nebraska Press.

Mihesuah, Devon Abbott, and Angela Cavender Wilson, eds. 2004. *Indigenizing the Academy: Transforming Scholarship and Empowering Communities.* Lincoln: University of Nebraska Press.

Mills, Antonia. 1994. *Eagle Down Is Our Law: Witsuwit'en Law, Feasts, and Land Claims.* Vancouver: UBC Press.

Mitchell, Chief Michael. 1989. 'An Unbroken Assertion of Sovereignty.' In Boyd Richardson, ed., *Drumbeat: Anger and Renewal in Indian Country.* Toronto: Summerhill Press.

Momaday, N. Scott. 1969. *The Way to Rainy Mountain.* Albuquerque: University of New Mexico Press.

– 1997. *The Man Made of Words.* New York: St Martin's Press.

Monet, Don, and Skanu'u (Ardythe Wilson). 1992. *Colonialism on Trial: Indigenous Land Rights and the Gitksan and Wet'suwet'en Sovereignty Case.* Gabriola Island, BC: New Society Publishers.

Monture-Angus, Patricia. 1999. *Journeying Forward: Dreaming First Nations' Independence.* Halifax, NS: Fernwood Publishing.

Morgan, Lewis Henry. 1993. *League of the Iroquois.* New York: Carol Publishing Group Edition.

Mulhall, Stephen, and Adam Swift. 1992. *Liberals and Communitarians.* Oxford: Blackwell.

Neihardt, John G. 1932. *Black Elk Speaks: Being the Life Story of a Holy Man of the Oglala Sioux, as Told through John G. Neihardt.* New York: William Morrow.

Office of Prime Minister Brian Mulroney. 1991 (27 August). *The Mandate: Royal Commission on Aboriginal Peoples, Background Documents.*

Paper, Jordan. 1988. *Offering Smoke: The Sacred Pipe and Indigenous Religion.* Boise: University of Idaho Press.

Parker, A.C. 1991. *The Constitution of the Five Nations or The Iroquois Book of the Great Law.* Ohsweken, ON.: Iroqrafts.

Persky, Stan. 1998. *Delgamuukw: The Supreme Court of Canada Decision on Aboriginal Title.* Vancouver, BC: Greystone Books.

Prucha, Francis Paul. 1984. *Great Father: The United States Government and the American Indians.* Vols. I and II. Lincoln: University of Nebraska Press.

Quine, W.V.O. 1980. 'Two Dogmas of Empiricism.' In *From a Logical Point of View: Nine Logico-Philosophical Essays.* Cambridge: Harvard University Press.

Rawls, John. 1971. *A Theory of Justice.* Cambridge MA: Harvard University Press.

– 1993. *Political Liberalism.* New York: Columbia University Press.

Richardson, Boyce, ed. 1989. *Drum Beat: Anger and Renewal in Indian Country.* Ottawa: Assembly of First Nations.

Rosenblum, Nancy. 1989. *Liberalism and the Moral Life.* Cambridge, MA: Harvard University Press.

Rotman, Leonard I. 1996. *Parallel Paths: Fiduciary Doctrine and the Crown-Native Relationship in Canada.* Toronto: University of Toronto Press.

Royal Commission on Aboriginal Peoples. 1993. *Partners in Confederation: Aboriginal Peoples, Self-Government, and the Constitution.* Ottawa: Minister of Supply and Services.

– 1995. *Treaty Making in the Spirit of Co-Existence: An Alternative to Extinguishment.* Ottawa: Minister of Supply and Services.

– 1996. *Report of the Royal Commission on Aboriginal Peoples.* 5 vols. Ottawa: Minister of Supply and Services.

Russell, Dan. 2000. *A People's Dream: Aboriginal Self-Government in Canada.* Vancouver: UBC Press.

Said, Edward. 1994. *Representations of the Intellectual.* New York: Vintage Books.

Sandel, Michael. 1982. *Liberalism and the Limits of Justice.* Cambridge: Cambridge University Press.

Simpson, Audra. 2003. 'To the Reserve and Back Again: Kahnawake Mohawk Narratives of Self, Home, and Nation.' PhD thesis, McGill University, Montreal.

Skinner, Quentin. 2003. *Visions of Politics.* 3 vols. Cambridge: Cambridge University Press.

Slattery, Brian. 1979. *The Land Rights of Indigenous Canadian Peoples.* Saskatoon: University of Saskatchewan Native Law Centre.

– 1983. *Ancestral Lands, Alien Laws: Judicial Perspectives on Aboriginal Title.*
Saskatoon: Native Law Centre, University of Saskatchewan.
– 1992. 'First Nations and the Constitution: A Question of Trust.' *Canadian Bar
Review* 71:26–93.
Smith, Linda Tuhiwai. 1999. *Decolonizing Methodologies: Research and Indigenous
Peoples.* New York: St Martin's Press.
Smith, Melvin H. 1995. *Our Home or Native Land? What Governments' Aboriginal
Policy Is Doing to Canada.* Victoria: Crown Western Press.
Snow, Dean R. 1996. *The Iroquois.* Oxford: Basil Blackwell.
Statement of the Government of Canada on Indian Policy. 1969. Ottawa: Queen's
Printer.
Taylor, Charles. 1990. *Sources of the Self.* Cambridge: Cambridge University
Press.
Tehanetorens. 1993. *Wampum Belts.* Ohsweken, ON: Iroqrafts.
Thomas, Chief Jake, and Terry Boyle. 1994. *Teachings from the Longhouse.*
Toronto: Stoddart Publishing.
Thompson, Janna. 2002. *Taking Responsibility for the Past: Reparation and Histori-
cal Injustice.* New York: Polity Press.
Tomasi, John. 2001. *Liberalism beyond Justice: Citizens, Society, and the Boundaries
of Political Theory.* Princeton, NJ: Princeton University Press.
Treaty 7 Elders and Tribal Council Walter Hidebrandt, Dorothy First Rider,
and Sarah Carter. 1996. *The True Spirit and Original Intent of Treaty 7.*
Montreal: McGill-Queen's University Press.
Trigger, Bruce, and Wilcomb Washburn, eds. 1995. *Cambridge History of the
Native Peoples of America.* Cambridge: Cambridge University Press.
Trudeau, Pierre Elliott. 1968. *Federalism and French Canadians.* New York: St
Martin's Press.
– 1970. *Approaches to Politics.* Toronto: University of Toronto Press.
– 1972. *Conversations with Canadians.* Toronto: University of Toronto Press.
Tully, James. 1993. *An Approach to Political Philosophy: Locke in Contexts.* Cam-
bridge: Cambridge University Press.
– 1995. *Strange Multiplicity: Constitutionalism in an Age of Diversity.* Cambridge:
Cambridge University Press.
– 2002. 'Political Philosophy as a Critical Activity.' *Political Theory* 30(4):535–55.
Turner, Dale. 2004a. 'Perceiving the World Differently.' In David Kahane and
Catherine Bell, eds., *Intercultural Dispute Resolution in Aboriginal Contexts:
Land Claims, Treaties, and Self-Government Agreements.* Vancouver: UBC Press.
– 2004b. 'Oral Traditions and the Politics of (Mis)Recognition.' In Anne
Waters, ed., *Amerindian Thought: Philosophical Essays.* Malden, MA:
Blackwell Publishing.

Turpel, Mary Ellen. 1993a. 'On the Question of Adapting the Canadian Criminal Justice System for Aboriginal Peoples: Don't Fence Me In.' In Royal Commission on Aboriginal Peoples, *Aboriginal Peoples and the Justice System*. Ottawa: Minister of Supply and Services. 161–83.

– 1993b. 'Patriarchy and Paternalism: The Legacy of the Canadian State for First Nations Women.' *Canadian Journal of Women and the Law* 6:174.

Union of British Columbia Indian Chiefs. 1970. *A Declaration of Indian Rights: The B.C. Indian Position Paper*. Victoria, BC: UBCIC.

Vennum, Thomas, jr. 1983. *Traditional Ojibwa Religion and Its Historical Changes*. Philadelphia, PA: American Philosophical Society.

Vizenor, Gerald. 1994. *Manifest Manners: Postindian Warriors of Survivance*. Hanover, NH: University Press of New England.

Wa, Gisday, and Delgam Uukw. 1992. *The Spirit in the Land: Statements of the Gitksan and Wet'suwet'en Hereditary Chiefs in the Supreme Court of British Columbia 1987–1990*. Gabriola, BC: Reflections.

Waldron, Jeremy. 1997. 'Superseding Historic Injustice.' *Ethics* 103:4–28.

– 2003. 'Indigeneity? First Peoples and Last Occupancy.' *The New Zealand Journal of Public and International Law* 1.

Wallace, Paul A. 1997. *The White Roots of Peace*. Santa Fe, NM: Clearlight Publishing.

Walzer, Michael. 1983. *Spheres of Justice: A Defense of Pluralism and Equality*. New York: Basic Books.

Warrior, Robert. 1995. *Tribal Secrets: Recovering Indian Intellectual Traditions*. Minneapolis: University of Minnesota Press.

Waubageshig. 1970. *The Only Good Indian: Essays by Canadian Indians*. Edmonton: Hurtig.

Weaver, Jace. 1997. *That the People Might Live: Native American Literatures and Native American Community*. New York: Oxford University Press.

Weaver, Sally. 1981. *Making Canadian Indian Policy: The Hidden Agenda 1968–70*. Toronto: University of Toronto Press.

Wilkins, David. 2002. *American Indian Politics and the American Political System*. Lanham, MD: Rowman & Littlefield.

Wilkinson, Charles. 2005. *Blood Struggle: The Rise of Modern Indian Nations*. New York: W.W. Norton.

Williams, Melissa S. 1998. *Voice, Trust, and Memory: Marginalized Groups and the Failings of Liberal Representation*. Princeton, NJ: Princeton University Press.

Williams, Robert A., Jr. 1992. *The American Indian in Western Legal Thought: The Discourses of Conquest*. Oxford: Oxford University Press.

Wittgenstein, Ludwig. 1990. *Tractacus Logico-Philosophicus*, trans. C.K. Ogden. New York: Routledge.

– 2001. *Philosophical Investigations*, trans. G.E.M. Anscombe. Malden, MA: Blackwell Press.

Wub-E-Ke-Niew. 1995. *We Have the Right to Exist*. New York: Black Thistle Press.

Wuttunee, William C. 1971. *Ruffled Feathers: Indians in Canadian Society*. Calgary, AB: Bell Books.

Young, Iris Marion. 1990. *Justice and the Politics of Difference*. Princeton, NJ: Princeton University Press.

– 2000. *Inclusion and Democracy*. Oxford: Oxford University Press.

Index

mutual recognition, 76–7; as complex
convention, 86; facets of, 77; in
constitutionalism, 85; *My Father's
House* (book), 97

narratives: indigenous, 50–1; spoken,
50; transcribing, 51
nation-states: indigenous cultures as,
36; Mohawk nationalism in, 110
nation-to-nation relationships, 40, 41,
94–5
National Committee on Indian
Rights and Treaties, 138, 139
National Indian Brotherhood, 27,
141
national minorities, incorporating,
59–60
nationalism: colonialism and indigenous, 109; indigenous, 110;
Mohawk, 110; as separatism, 107
nationalist, Alfred as indigenous, 106
nationhood: bestowed by Two Row
Wampum, 54–5; defined, 79;
European concept of, 36; indigenous understandings of, 79;
negotiating the meaning of, 110;
protesting indigenous, 106
Native American studies programs,
evolution of, 105
Native Council of Canada, 27
Native law, as specialty, 90. *See also*
law
Native Rights in Canada (book), 19
Native Women's Association of
Canada, 27
nature, in renewal concept, 50
Neihardt, John G., 100
Nishga Indian Tribal Council, seeks
land title, 21
Nisga'a First Nation, 21

Ojibway lands, *St. Catherine's Milling*
case, 18–19
Oka crisis, 80
oral histories: legal use of, 82
oral traditions, indigenous, 45–7, 51;
rights rooted in, 84; world view, 81
oratory, in diplomacy, 47
ownership: Aboriginal rights approach to, 4; and sovereignty, 5

parallelism model, 40
participation, Aboriginal, 7; in
Canadian affairs, 112; defined, 31;
desirability, 93; equal, 126–7; as key
to survival, 11; in legal and political discourse, 72; in mainstream
academia, 106; and tension within
communities, 95; Tully view of
value of, 73–4; in White Paper, 125
'Passing of the Pipe' (poem), 1
peace, Iroquois assumptions of, 53
Peace, Power and Righteousness (book),
107
peaceful coexistence, 85
person, defined as non–Indian, 12
philosophers, Aboriginal: dialogue
with European, 100; roles of, 114;
as teachers, 114; views summarized, 119; word warriors compared, 120
philosophers, European, 113–14;
dialogue with aboriginal, 100;
discourse about Aboriginal people,
69
philosophies: African forms, 97;
flaws in comparing European and
indigenous, 102; text in, 47; varia-
tions in European, 100
philosophy, 117; diversity in indigenous, 10; requirements for critical